Making Mediation
Your Day Job

Making Mediation Your Day Job

How to Market Your ADR
Business Using Mediation
Principles You Already Know

Tammy Lenski, Ed.D.

iUniverse, Inc.
New York   Bloomington

Making Mediation Your Day Job

iUniverse books may be ordered through booksellers or by contacting:

iUniverse
1663 Liberty Drive
Bloomington, IN 47403
www.iuniverse.com
1-800-Authors (1-800-288-4677)

Because of the dynamic nature of the Internet, any Web addresses or
links contained in this book may have changed since publication and
may no longer be valid. The views expressed in this work are solely those
of the author and do not necessarily reflect the views of the publisher,
and the publisher hereby disclaims any responsibility for them.

ISBN: 978-1-935278-88-7 (pbk)
ISBN: 978-1-935278-89-4 (ebk)

Library of Congress Control Number: 2009911123

Printed in the United States of America

iUniverse rev. date: 11/5/2009

For Rod

My Man from the Midwest,
who gave me space,
who never doubted my dreams,
who fills my life with light.

Contents

Acknowledgments ix

Introduction xi

Chapter 1:   Market like a Mediator 1

Chapter 2:   Marketing from a Mediation Frame of Mind 11

Chapter 3:   Creating Space for the Important 20

Chapter 4:   Narrowing Your Market 31

Chapter 5:   Uncovering Interests 45

Chapter 6:   Reframing How You Help 52

Chapter 7:   Building Dialogue with Your Market 68

Chapter 8:   Setting Your Practice-Building Agenda 96

Recommended Resources 107

References 109

Acknowledgments

The creation of any work of substance is not a lonely pursuit. It is an act of collaboration with all the minds and hearts of those with whom the author crossed paths, both before and during the creation.

My faculty colleagues at Woodbury College—Alice, Susan, David, Gary, Jen, and Lynn—warm my heart, help me raise my craft to new levels, and keep me humble in the presence of true collegiality and elegant mediation skill. My current and former students ask the questions that create fodder for my writing and reflecting and make me a better teacher and trainer in the process. Without them helping me realize the need, this book would never have been born.

The readers of my MediatorTech.com blog were a blessing, because many of them took the time to leave comments and send e-mails with feedback as I blogged large sections of the second draft. They told me what made sense, what raised their consciousness, what ticked them off, and what tickled their fancy. They told me what gave them greater insight into and easier anticipation of marketing. And four of my former students, Christine, Jasmine, Scott, and Judy, gave a great deal of specific feedback that helped me keep—or get back—on track. They managed to be kind and direct at the same time.

My big sister Harriet (Pepi to me) has read my blog from day one, though she's neither a mediator nor a techie. She's a sister who cares. And she read with the head and heart of a small business owner, so her e-mailed notes about posts that stood out helped provide some of the earliest content for this book. She has a heart as big as any I've ever known.

And then there's Rod, who's never once doubted my ability to accomplish whatever I set my mind to, even when I did. When I walked in the door in 1997 and announced I wanted to resign my well-paid, influential, fulfilling job and go into business as a mediator, he only blinked once (at least in my presence), then launched himself into finding ways to adapt our lives to my new dream. He did it again on the day I said, "I'm going to write a book," and every day thereafter. Making mediation my day job happened in large part because I have a partner who cares as much about my dreams as I do.

Introduction

A confluence of three events lead to this book.

The first was the initial class of my advanced-level course, Trends and Issues in the Field. To spark discussion about the relevance of social trends to the practice of mediation, I asked my graduate mediation students to work in small groups and address this scenario:

> Imagine that you have decided to create a private ADR (alternative dispute resolution) practice. How would you go about getting work and building business?

The small groups took their markers and flipcharts and disappeared for 45 minutes. As I paused at the doors of the breakout rooms in which they worked, I could see earnest and diligent conversation unfolding, words appearing on paper. These were groups of smart adult students who came to grad school often on the heels of successful careers in other arenas.

The small groups returned and hung their lists on walls around the room. My eyes skimmed the posters. I was sure I'd missed something that surely had to be there. I skimmed them again.

These smart people had produced a thorough and exhaustive list of the formal programs, panels, and volunteer mediation opportunities that now exist in many states, including court-, government- and community-associated ADR. Every group's list included options like these:

- Find out if my state's Postal Service roster is accepting new mediators.

- Contact the courts to find out what mediation panels are recruiting mediators.

- Contact my state's child welfare agencies about child guardianship and permanency adoption programs.

- Call my local community mediation centers and volunteer in order to build my portfolio.

Every approach sought to acquire work from a program that already existed and was run by someone else. Noticeably absent were any practice-building or client-generating strategies to be conducted by these mediators on their own behalf.

I was floored, frankly. My class notes from that day, with double underlines, say, "We need to do a far better job of conveying to students, early in the program, that reliance on existing programs for work means unlikely success as a private mediator."

By the time I attended a regional ADR conference about a month later, I had mused quite a bit about that first day of class. Was such thinking somehow limited to our grad students, I wondered, or was their thinking typical of others in the field?

At the conference, I made a point of asking my fellow mediators a version of the same question: *Where do you turn to catch new waves of opportunity for building your ADR practice?*

My anecdotal, informal research yielded responses that were uncannily similar and now too familiar ... it wasn't just my grad students.

Getting beyond Neutrality

I was considering Bernard Mayer's *Beyond Neutrality: Confronting the Crisis in Conflict Resolution* as a text for one of my upcoming classes and began rereading it soon after the conference. But this time, I read with those two experiences rattling about in my brain.

In his important book, Mayer paints a compelling portrait of a field in danger of stalled development. He makes a strong case that ours is still primarily a supply-driven field that hasn't successfully engaged the public's ongoing interest or consciousness. Mayer points out, rightly so, that we haven't been meaningfully included in some of the most important conflicts of our time and are too frequently left on the outside of conflicts, even in our own communities.

He proposes that we have become over-committed to the ideas of neutrality and resolution and have failed to understand the public's suspicion of, or disinterest in, these basic tenets. He argues that we should be framing our work—both for ourselves and certainly for the public—as conflict engagement instead of conflict resolution:

> If we can genuinely liberate ourselves in all that we do from this resolution bias—that is, from the automatic assumption that our role is to bring about resolution—and instead see our role as helping people engage constructively in all phases of the conflict process, then our ability to have a constructive impact on conflict will dramatically increase.—Bernard Mayer, *Beyond Neutrality*

Mayer has suggested that the developmental crisis isn't so much the result of inadequate marketing as of practitioners' failure, as a whole, to offer our skills and talents in services that are truly compelling to the public.

As I considered Mayer's words in light of recent conversations with my grad students and fellow conference-goers, I realized that ADR's developmental crisis is much more closely associated to inadequate marketing than Mayer suggests.

Many mediators I've met are hesitant marketers. If you were drawn to *Making Mediation Your Day Job*, you may be among them. The field is struggling, in part, because many of its professionals aren't yet building healthy individual practices by using leading-edge approaches already well utilized in other successful service fields. When I discuss marketing with mediators, I notice a dislike of "selling myself" and a hesitation to use online technology for creating real leverage. Out-of-date marketing methods—or worse, little real marketing at all—result in a public that's woefully unfamiliar with how you can help.

More important, truly effective marketing, in today's terms, means that you learn from your market and adjust your services accordingly. When you engage your market in a two-way conversation, you listen and learn. You give yourself the opportunity to really understand what they want and in what form. In other words, when you market well, you address Mayer's concerns about over-reliance on resolution and neutrality, because your market will tell you what they want and need.

If you mediate because you want to help people navigate conflict more successfully, how do you know that Mediation (the formal process) is the best way to deliver on your purpose? When you engage in dialogue fully, you open yourself to new information that may well change how you do what you do.

A Case of Outmoded Marketing

Around the same time, I noticed an increase in the number of calls and e-mails I was receiving from my fellow mediators.

"I've heard you have a full-time practice, and I'd like to see if I can pick your brain," said one typical e-mail. Another said, "I'm on a plateau with my business and am beginning to panic a bit about the lack of income. I sure could use some help getting pointed in the right direction."

As I talked with mediators from around the United States, I started to see a pattern in the challenges most of them faced.

Many approached marketing with distaste. Few were truly comfortable with the online environment and the ways they could leverage it to help build their practices. Even fewer seemed to have laid a solid foundation for launching their marketing strategies ... if they even had a marketing strategy.

It wasn't, I realized, anything to do with intelligence or business savvy.

It seemed to be associated with an outmoded way of looking at marketing.

The Questions This Book Answers

The seeds for this book were planted, and in the coming months I pondered questions that grew from that class activity and my many subsequent conversations with mediators attempting to build successful private practices:

Why are many mediators looking for work primarily through opportunities someone else has created? Perhaps mediators who tried to build business and found very few clients coming through the door believe the chance for any work at all is better than spinning private-practice wheels. The trouble is, of course, that only a few mediators make a real living through rosters and panels, and the more who want in, the less work there is for all involved. The pay scale of most rosters also makes it difficult to thrive.

Why aren't mediators tuning into real market needs and capitalizing on them? It is as though the real opportunities are somehow invisible. Perhaps the idea of creating something new feels daunting, or perhaps new mediators want the credibility and legitimacy that panel affiliations seem to give them. Yet the time and effort they put into these affiliations drains from time to successfully build a practice that's independent of such affiliation.

How can more mediators experience the synergy of thinking like an entrepreneur? Is it possible that some mediators dislike marketing so much that they prefer to rely on already-existing programs to send them a thin trickle of work? If this is true, then it's not surprising that so many mediators can more rightly call their work a hobby than a business.

How can those of us who educate and train mediators do a better job of helping our participants and graduates step outside the limiting confines of community, government, and court-based programs? This seems especially important if we are to address increasingly vocal criticism about turning more mediators loose in a field that has too many mediators still trying to make a living by mediating.

This book is my response to these questions. It's written for mediators with a passion for helping people successfully navigate conflict, but with considerably less passion for marketing. It's written to create the foundation needed in order to use online marketing strategies effectively. It's the kind of manual I wish I'd had when I founded my practice over a decade ago, and the kind that mediators I teach and work with today tell me they want.

Stop Waiting, Start Building

If you believe that mediation should primarily be the business of the courts, or something you give away as a gift from your heart, you can stop reading here— this book will do little for you. If you don't believe those things, then you must do the following instead:

Stop putting most of your effort into applications to ADR panels and rosters. You are not likely to earn enough from these positions, because there are not enough of them for all the professionals who want to make mediation their day job and panel-obtained mediations do not tend to pay sufficiently for a mediator to live on.

Stop banking on a living wage from state agency referrals and rosters. Even in states with healthy mediation programs associated with government agencies, there will not be enough work to pay you and all the other mediators clamoring for a piece of the pie.

Stop giving most of the time you have available to develop your practice to your community mediation center in the name of getting experience. Give them some of your time, as community mediation centers play an important role, but keep a significant portion of your time for serious development of your practice.

Stop waiting for referrals from lawyers. Many attorneys like to refer ADR work to other attorneys because that's the dispute resolution world they know best. Even if you're an attorney, it's going to take a long time to build a full-time practice that way.

Stop waiting for your national, regional, and state associations to educate the public and create work for you. Most of our associations don't have enough per-son-power or fiscal resources to make this a reality any time soon. And it's debat-able whether that should even be their job.

If you're doing much of the above, you're doing what I call "*Field of Dreams* marketing": build it, and hope they will come.

Stop waiting for someone else. Start creating your own reality, in just the way you expect your mediation clients to take responsibility for their own lives, behaviors, and decisions. You can make the commitment to start right now.

Overwhelmed and Turned Off

When I founded my full-time private practice in 1997, I had no prior entrepreneurial experience and wasn't particularly savvy about business ownership. I was a college vice president and dean at the time, and though I had lots of experience managing people, managing large budgets, and administering a decentralized organization (not to mention lots of experience as an "insider" mediator), I had never thought of myself as an entrepreneur or businessperson.

I became a business owner because I wanted, more than anything, to make mediation my day job.

When I began educating myself about marketing and building a business, I initially felt overwhelmed and turned off by some of the counsel I received. Business development advisors told me I'd need to invest in advertising, schmooze a great deal at business networking events, and learn how to be a good salesperson. Several advised me to master the art of cold calling. It was that latter piece of advice that prompted me to sit in my shiny new office one afternoon, blue as can be.

I knew that if I had to do many of these tasks, I'd fail. It just wasn't me, and I wasn't interested in transforming myself into someone who could do those tasks. I knew that if I had to cold call people and try to convince them I had something they really needed, I'd never do it. I knew that if I followed the ABCs of sales, "Always be closing," I'd feel like a fraud. I realized that if I had to do many of the things traditionally associated with marketing and sales, I simply wouldn't do them, and my business would flounder before it ever gained real traction.

I'm not one for hovering long in powerless places or giving up easily on a dream. So I decided to do something different than what I had been advised. I decided to market my ADR practice based on my strengths and the kinds of tasks I enjoy.

This book is about the simple and effective system I developed from studying, experimenting, and thinking about marketing from the mediator's chair. It's a book that I hope will change the way you think about the business of mediation, help you find your footing in the field, and inspire you to think of practice development in ways that build instead of sap your energy.

It's a book about building on what you already know and value in order to do the work you love.

A Few Words on My Terminology Choice

You have, no doubt, noticed that I use the phrase "making mediation your day job," not "making ADR your day job." Mediation is used in the literature of our field to refer to a specific dispute resolution process that carries certain elements distinguishing it from other processes such as arbitration, facilitation, negotiation, neutral evaluation, and the like. In my classroom, I would call this—with a generous nod to Jennifer Beer and Eileen Stief—big "M" mediation.

For this book, I have chosen "mediation" for its small "m" connotation, one that I fear is getting lost in the adjunctification of mediation to the legal field. Small "m" mediation encompasses the myriad distinguishable formal processes that bring a *mediative influence* on conflict.

You will notice, as you read on, that I do not use "attorney-mediator" and "non-attorney-mediator" terminology in the book. Each is a problematic phrase and contributes to public confusion that further hobbles the development of the field. I invite you to stop using these terms, too.

The term "attorney-mediator" suggests that the two professional roles are performed simultaneously or that one is necessarily an adjunct of the other. Either interpretation risks a conclusion by an ill-informed public that the two go hand-in-hand. Such a suggestion fails to honor the historical roots of this field and the significant number of excellent mediators who hail from other professional backgrounds.

Adopting "attorney-mediator" language necessitates other hybrids in order to be inclusive and fairly acknowledge the rich diversity of backgrounds: therapist-mediator, educator-mediator, social-worker-mediator, physician-mediator. The list would become exhausting before it could become exhaustive and would drift into the ridiculous: horse-trainer-mediator, massage-therapist-mediator and so on.

The term "non-attorney-mediator" is at best confusing and at worst insulting. It defines mediators who have degrees other than a J.D. by the absence of attorney-ness. It is the equivalent of referring to African Americans, Native Americans, Latin Americans, and others who are not Caucasian by the term "non-White." No one should be defined by what they are not. "Non-attorney-mediator" is a marginalizing term and, accordingly, has no place in our field.

Instead, I have chosen to use the term "professional mediator," which is not without deficiencies of its own. It's a term I chose to embrace all mediators who wish to make mediation their day job, without regard to profession of origin, academic degree, and preparatory history.

How to Get the Most from This Book

You could read this book in a single evening, but I hope you won't.

It's designed to be concise and more like a pocket guide than a tome of wisdom. It's formatted with each major point creating its own section so that you have space for notes and can find an idea again quickly. But its length and formatting has nothing to do with encouraging speed-reading.

Instead, I hope its brevity and layout encourages you to take your time and know that you can move through it with care because you won't be overwhelmed with complexity or wordiness.

Much of the book is designed to be interactive. To get the most from it, I invite you to *engage* the book instead of simply reading it. We know from the latest learning research conducted by neuropsychologists that actively engaging reading material significantly improves retention and the ability to apply it. Engage it by jotting notes in the white space I've provided. By flagging (with sticky notes or sticky tabs, for instance) pages you want to return to for further reflection. By jotting down your questions or insights on those sticky notes.

This book is of little use to you if you don't apply it to your practice.

With this in mind, I've crafted most chapters to close with reflective questions that tease out your thinking and begin the process of applying my system to your own mediation practice.

I recommend that you create a computer file or purchase a journal-style notebook just for the purpose of working through this book. In so doing, you'll create a special place for your practice-building efforts to take shape, which will hold your hopes and dreams for the work you love. By taking the time to write down your responses to the reflective questions, you'll begin building momentum in your marketing efforts, and you'll have the physical evidence of that momentum right in front of your eyes.

The exercises are designed to build on one another and create direction and momentum for you over time. Some exercises will take fewer than five minutes; others may be ones you ponder for several days before completing. I encourage you to take the time you need to flesh out your thinking in an exercise. It's likely you'll return to some exercises to refine over time.

Are you ready to make mediation your day job?

CHAPTER 1

Market like a Mediator

The wise man doesn't give the right answers, he poses the right questions.—Claude Levi-Strauss

Transformation comes more from pursuing profound questions than seeking practical answers.—Peter Block

Confidence, like art, never comes from having all the answers; it comes from being open to all the questions.—Earl Gray Stevens

Like any mediator worth her salt, I don't have the right answers for you. But I do know how to ask good questions that will help you find your own best answers.

Your path toward success in your mediation business isn't just a matter of finding the right answers from other people who've succeeded, though they'll certainly have some hints that could work for you, too. It's a matter of finding the best answers to some of the most important questions you can ask yourself about your business, your dreams, and your way of helping make the world a better place.

That I can do. I can help you ask the right questions at the right time to set yourself in the right direction for success.

I can do for you what I can do for my mediation clients: Offer an approach to exploring a problem that creates the right circumstances for new insights on which you can take action.

Throughout this book, I'll approach our work here as a mediator approaches her work. And in so doing, I hope to be able to demonstrate what it means to market like a mediator.

You already know how, actually.

Hopefully, Not a Self-Help Book

I admit it: I struggle with self-help books. You can probably see that already.

I struggle with the sheer volume *of* them on the shelves of my local independent bookstore. I struggle with the sheer volume *in* them, so much wisdom packed into the pages that I can't absorb it fully. I struggle with the hype and the preaching in some of them. And I struggle with the idea that their way, according to some self-help authors, should be *my* way.

Sometimes it should be my way. Sometimes it shouldn't.

I struggle with advice because my mediator education and experience have taught me to be extraordinarily cautious about giving advice to people whose lives I'm part of for just a sliver of time. Like yours.

So I set out to write a marketing self-help book for mediators that isn't really a self-help book. I'm not subscribing to a set of techniques. I'm not offering you The System That Will Transform Your Mediation Business. I'm not telling you that if you do it my way, you will thrive. How could I possibly know that? I'm not interested in hyping you into following My Path.

How will you use this book to move your practice forward in the way a mediator helps parties move forward?

Bridge the Gap

I also struggle with self-help books because, as a mediation professor and conflict resolution trainer, I've crossed paths with thousands of people who have consumed such books with a strong desire to change something in their lives, but their lives haven't really changed.

I've also talked to a lot of mediators who want to make mediation their day job and own a veritable library of marketing and blogging books, but still struggle to pay the bills or earn enough to leave their current day job.

What I've seen is how difficult it is to inhabit the Gap—the distance between what we intellectually know and what we actually do. Hard stuff, that. My doctoral dissertation examined human behavior change, and bridging the Gap can be elusive indeed.

I've tried not to write a mediation marketing self-help book that will leave you without a bridge across that Gap. This book is the bridge.

What do you need to create your own bridge to span the Gap?

The Bridge across the Gap

What builds a strong bridge across the Gap? Here's my list:

Using what you already know to leverage what you want to achieve. Mediators already know how to build businesses successfully in today's marketplace because we already know and work daily with some of the key concepts that have the marketing world abuzz. They're old news to us. The new news is using them not just when we're in the mediator's chair but also when we are trying to create more opportunities to be in the mediator's chair.

Keeping it simple. I've edited this book seven times, and I've been merciless with myself. I don't want you to have another tome so clogged with information that you can't digest it all. I want to offer a simple, concise set of ideas that inspire you to action and suggest some launching points and direction. This little book is deliberately brief in order to hold me to that goal so that you can reach yours.

Getting comfortable with discomfort. The Gap is the place where your discomfort meets your comfort, where what you know meets what you do. I think the approach you'll read in future chapters minimizes marketing discomfort substantially, but it doesn't erase it. You'll need to find in yourself the courage to step onto the bridge.

Choosing mind frame over technique. I'll let a former mediation student of mine, Kate, describe this one to you.

Before that, though, what will make a strong bridge for you?

It Was a Light Bulb Moment

Interpersonal Conflict class with my mediation students was just getting underway when Kate raised her hand. "May I tell a quick story about something that happened this morning? I promise it's relevant to class!" Kate seemed so excited, so electrified, that it was impossible to say no.

"I got into an argument with my husband this morning," she began. "It wasn't about anything dire, just daily little stuff. I thought to myself, *I'll put my good mediator skills to use and make this conversation go better!* So I did all the right things: I reflected back, I asked good questions, I uncovered interests, I reframed. I was so proud of myself!

"But there was one little problem. It was making things worse. The more I did my mediator stuff, the angrier my husband seemed to get. At first I thought he was just being petty because it was clear that I was handling myself so much better than he was handling himself.

"But then it hit me. I was using my good skills for an evil purpose! I was using them with the intent of making him see it *my* way. And the more I backed my husband into the corner I wanted him in, the harder he worked to get out, the angrier he got, and the more downhill the conversation went.

"It was such a light bulb moment for me, Tammy," she concluded. "That's when I finally really got it. All the good conflict management skills in the world are only truly effective when they're used with the right intention."

How will you create the right intentions for your marketing instead of simply applying technique?

Frame of Mind Matters

As Kate's story illustrates, techniques don't get you very far. They can look and feel artificial. And the desire to apply them correctly can distract you from being mentally present in the way you want to be.

It's like taking a mediation training course, trying to mimic your trainer's phrases, and over-relying on the mediation anatomy when you're in the mediator's chair. You end up not sounding like yourself and becoming confused about where you are. In basic mediation trainings, I'm regularly asked, "Can you just tell me what I should say/do in circumstances like this one? If you can just tell me, I'll do it."

If Kate's right—and it's what I've been successfully teaching clients for years, so I obviously believe she is—then the way you think about marketing influences how you act as a marketer. Instead of dutifully subscribing to a set of techniques, if you adopt an effective way to think about it, you'll have greater success with it.

So if you want to make mediation your day job, your first act must be to ensure that your marketing frame of mind will be effective for you and your business. How will you do that?

Mediation Mind Frame Marketing

The heart of the marketing questions you'll be asked in this book have their origins in concepts you already use as a mediator. If you know how to mediate well, then you're well situated to find effective answers to the questions that are your marketing building blocks. That's because all you'll need to do is extend your thinking about the application of those concepts beyond the world of mediation and into the world of practice building.

If you're new to mediation and still learning to master the craft, then you can cultivate your good mediator skills right alongside your good marketing skills and still get going with the explorations ahead. These explorations will help you learn more about mediation.

Let's start right now. Many mediators work from the assumption and belief that the parties know best what will work for them and can sort out their dispute if we, the mediators, can help clear the debris out of their way.

If you're a mediator who works from this orientation, then you help people explore, uncover, consider, and reflect. You come to them as a guide instead of as an expert who knows what they should do and how they should do it.

That's the spirit with which I will work with you over the course of this book. Just as when I mediate, I will attempt to clear away debris, reframe the problems you're trying to solve with your marketing, raise questions for your consideration, and help guide you in your own thinking. I won't try to give you a recipe for success, but will instead offer you a compass and a few essential navigational ideas from which to set course.

Just as in effective conflict management, you'll be asked to try ideas on for size, experiment with options, reality test ideas, and ultimately choose what's best for you as the expert in your own life and business.

I call it Mediator Mind Frame Marketing because if you can think like a mediator not just when you're in the mediator's chair but also when you're marketing, you're on your way.

What could happen if you could take the way you think when you're in the mediation chair and use it when you're in the marketer's chair?

Not a Single New Idea

There's not a single new idea in this book.

The mediation concepts aren't new.

The marketing concepts aren't new. Some of them may be new-ish. Or new to you, perhaps.

I'm less an inventor than a synthesizer. I'm a fan of synthesizing seemingly disparate ideas into formulations that create new energy for folks who make use of them. That's what I do as a mediator. That's what I do as an educator. And that's what I'm doing in this book.

So in this book I've tried to take some not-new ideas and commingle them in such a way that mediators who don't like or don't know much about marketing may discover they really *do*.

Do you dislike marketing? Do you think you don't know enough about it? What if those assumptions were wrong?

Reflective Question 1.1
Is there a gap between what you know about marketing and what you do?

If there is, describe the gap as best you can so that you can clearly see it in your mind's eye. If you don't think there is, consider an alternate version of the question: Do you do all the marketing tasks you know or suspect you should do?

Reflective Question 1.2
If there is a gap, what will it take for you to bridge it?

This is a hard question disguised as a simple one. Don't skip it. If you start skipping questions in the first chapter, you're setting an ineffective pattern for the rest of the book. Take a break, think about it, come back, and take a pass at an answer.

Reflective Question 1.3
What questions has this chapter raised for you?

Because as a mediator your stock in trade, like mine, is asking good questions, I'm guessing you've already found some bubbling to the surface. Let's not lose them. Jot them down now.

CHAPTER 2

Marketing from a Mediation Frame of Mind

The greatest challenge to any thinker is stating the problem in a way that will allow a solution.—Bertrand Russell

Metaphoric reframing attempts to find a new or altered metaphor for describing a situation or concept, thus changing the way in which it is viewed.—Bernard Mayer

It turns out that an effective mediation marketing frame of mind is not unlike an effective mediator's frame of mind. It's made up of components like these:

- Curiosity
- Willingness to try new ideas
- Comfort with not knowing
- Humility

It also values the same kinds of methods that mediation is widely recognized as valuing:

- Dialogue
- Self-determination
- Mutually satisfying outcomes

And it's made up of characteristics like those offered by Daniel Bowling and David Hoffman to describe "mediator presence":

- Being centered
- Being connected to one's governing values and beliefs and highest purpose
- Making contact with the humanity of others
- Being congruent

In essence, if you're a mediator (or want to be one), then this mediation marketing frame of mind probably feels familiar to you, like a favorite sweater that still holds your body shape when you take it off.

A mediation marketer's frame of mind is distinctly different from a traditional marketer's frame of mind. Instead of disliking marketing or finding yourself less effective at it than you'd like, a mediation marketing frame of mind feels like coming home.

Why Some Mediators Dislike Marketing … For Good Reasons

Not all mediators dislike marketing or approach it ineffectively, of course. If you're reading this book, it possible that there are a few things about marketing that you're looking to strengthen and some marketing tasks you wouldn't miss if they magically disappeared tomorrow. Here are the most common reasons mediators tell me they shy away from, dislike, or downright can't stand marketing:

When marketing is like over-cooked spinach. If you're of a certain age and went through U.S. public schools, you'll recall cafeteria monitors who made sure you ate all the food on your little orange elementary school cafeteria tray. Remember the odorous little pile of overcooked spinach, left for last because it closely resembled something no human should be forced to ingest?

With how much zest did you eat the cafeteria vegetable you despised?

Maybe you finally ate it, grimacing in disgust with every slither down your throat. Or maybe you pinched your nostrils shut with one hand while shoveling the offending vegetable in with the other, swallowing as fast as you could to get it over with. Or maybe, like me, you had regular showdowns with the cafeteria monitor, obstinately refusing to eat that awful little bowl of food.

For some, the act of "doing marketing" is akin to stinky, overcooked cafeteria spinach. You do it dutifully, but try to get it over with as quickly as possible. Or you grind your teeth in distaste all the while. Or you simply don't do much of it at all.

When marketing is like pitching, and you can't throw. Let's head back to primary school again. I'll try to keep the trauma minimal.

It's time for gym, and the game of the day is baseball. Imagine that you can't throw to save your life, but you're pretty darn handy with the mitt. You've been put on a team for the next two months, and the team with the most wins will get special awards at a school assembly at the end of the year. The gym teacher appoints you as pitcher. Your heart sinks.

How much are you looking forward to gym for the next two months?

For some, marketing asks you to play to your weaknesses instead of your strengths. Instead of being assigned a role that has you looking forward to gym, you drag your heels going down the hall and develop a sudden stomachache that yields a pass to the school nurse and a blessed reprieve from all-too-public failure.

If you associate marketing with cold calling or schmoozing at your local business networking group's monthly meetings, and you're not interested in or good at either, you're going to drag your heels. Maybe you even feel that stomachache coming on even as you read phrases like "cold calling."

When marketing is like selling used cars. I recall a used car salesman who ran tacky commercials on one of my local television affiliates years ago. The commercials were the kind of quality often associated with low-budget ads. The salesman wore a weird red wig that reminded me of my childhood Raggedy Andy doll. The car salesman's tagline was, "I won't stop wearing this wig until I convince you to buy a car from me!"

For some, marketing is associated with hype, hyperbole, and hyperactivity. Perhaps you associate it with being manipulated, having something put over on you, or even being lied to. These days, that kind of marketing meets with skepticism and resistance from a public worn out by the Raggedy Andy car salesmen. If you're a mediator who associates marketing with this kind of activity, then you're going to steer clear.

And for good reason. You just wouldn't look good in a red Raggedy Andy wig.

If marketing is like overcooked spinach, you're going to avoid it. If marketing is like pitching when you can't throw, you're going to dislike every moment on the mound. You may begin to enjoy as you get better at it, but you'll still feel frustration if the way you're marketing isn't yielding results. And if marketing is like selling used cars, you're going to feel slimy every time you sit down to do dreaded "M word" tasks.

Those perceptions are outdated and outmoded, and they belong in the outhouse. Mediators who dislike or fear marketing tend to approach the building of a marketing plan with these kinds of questions:

- How can I make myself do more traditional marketing? That's like asking, How can I get more of that yummy, overcooked spinach?

- Why do some people do this so well, but I'm getting such poor results? That's like asking, Why can't I just be a better pitcher?

- How can I get more comfortable with being a slick salesman? That's like asking, Do you have a Raggedy Andy wig I can borrow?

Ask Yourself Better Questions

As a mediator, you know this already: Ineffective questions lead to less effective answers. If the questions above are similar to the questions you ask yourself about marketing, it's time to ask yourself different questions. If you need a Marketing Monitor, like one of those cafeteria monitors, to stand over you and make sure you do your marketing tasks, you're in trouble before you even begin.

Instead of trying to change yourself into whatever perception you have of "a marketer," let's change how you think of marketing into a set of mind frames and approaches to which you're drawn, heart and soul. Instead of trying to guess what marketing secret you don't know, let's build your marketing on a set of concepts you already know and value.

What are *your* better questions?

Practice Building Is No Time to Be Neutral

During a conversation with a mediator in the Midwestern United States, I listened as she described her marketing efforts to date. She has regularly advertised in her local daily, buys an annual yellow pages quarter-column ad, has a traditional website that was professionally designed, sends out a print newsletter quarterly, and has a few other traditional strategies in her informal marketing plan. After two years in practice, she's not coming close to making a living.

During the conversation, I asked her how she communicates her passion for ADR and its benefits to her prospective clients and audience. There was a long silence. Then she said, "As a mediator, I believe it's my responsibility to convey neutrality and professional distance. Passion doesn't really enter into it."

Ah. It's the Mediator Neutrality Trap!

If you're a mediator who hesitates to convey your passion for what you do, you've taken the concepts of neutrality and professional distance way too much to heart. As I noted in the introduction, the field has also taken the commitment to neutrality too far, and that's a hard enough course correction. If you carry your mediator neutrality with you like a shield, the distance you keep yourself from your market will be detrimental to your practice's health.

It's critical that you get beyond neutrality when you market. There is no room for neutrality unless you also want your prospective clients to feel neutral about *you*.

What do you feel passion about?

Work from Your Strengths

If you're like most people, you probably play to your strengths much of the time. After all, your strengths carry you while you shore up your growing edges. For many mediators, the actions typically associated with traditional marketing feel more like they play to your weaknesses, or at least to your misgivings and self-doubts.

Let's consider this through a conflict lens. Engaging conflict is hard because, at least in some ways, it calls upon you to confront your fears. Conflict may press your buttons because you experience a real or perceived threat to some part of your identity: your view of yourself as competent, autonomous, worthy of being included, and so on.

You may find marketing a challenge for similar reasons. Offering your talents for the world to buy or ignore puts your identity on the line. Mediocre (or bad) results from your marketing efforts imply judgments by others of your competence or value.

Kat, a new professional in the field, put it this way: "I'm already resistant to doing the kinds of things that most marketing books tell me I need to do. So, when I do them and then don't see results, two things happen. I dislike doing those tasks even more next time. And my dislike of the tasks shines through to the very people I'm trying to reach. It's like a double slap in the face."

No more slapping yourself in the face! Building a marketing strategy based on your strengths yields four immediate, compelling, and irresistible results:

- You'll do it better.

- You'll enjoy it more.

- You'll more likely follow through because it's enjoyable.

- You'll attract others to you because you're working from your passion.

Marketing from your strengths doesn't completely release you from all tasks that fail to capitalize on what you do best. But it does mean that the bulk of your marketing tasks should be based on your strengths in order to build momentum from which to launch your less desirable tasks.

What are your strengths, both related and unrelated to ADR?

On Being a Good Mediator

Perhaps it goes without saying, but one of those strengths should be mediation.

Even the most magical marketing strategy will not counterbalance mediocre mediation skills. The most successful practices create momentum from word-of-mouth referrals, and it takes quality work to motivate prior clients to help you find new ones. In the end, it's the quality of the work you deliver that's going to help keep the clients coming.

I believe that the real move forward for our profession will come, in part, from development of higher practice standards. While there are a few people in the world who need little formal training to be good mediators, this is simply not the case for most of us.

It's called "basic mediation" for a reason, and there are few other occupations involving intervention in people's lives and behaviors where practitioners have the equivalent of one workweek's (or less) training. We will be taken seriously when we begin to take our own development and education seriously.

Building a successful practice, then, is two-pronged: Learn how to market well, and continuously improve your mediation skills.

When you think you know all you need to know, remind yourself of the learning stages model I first heard about back in graduate school during the 1980s, which has been attributed to a number of sources going as far back as the 1970s.

Stage 1: Unconscious incompetence. The learner is not yet adequately aware of what they don't know (This would be a common stage for mediators who have completed a basic mediation workshop and have not yet had any additional training).

Stage 2: Conscious incompetence. The learner begins to become aware of what they don't yet know.

Stage 3: Conscious competence. With study, practice, and commitment, the learner has developed essential competence in the new arena, but practice of the new skills remains a conscious, focused task to achieve success.

Stage 4: Unconscious competence. The learner has experienced "the zone" or a state of flow in which self-conscious attention has been replaced by outwardly directed mastery (Beware: New mediators may mistake a few moments of decent work with the true mastery of this stage).

At what stage are you?

Reflection Question 2.1
What mediator values and beliefs would you like to carry with you into your marketing work?

One way to approach this question is to first list the values, beliefs, and principles you hold dear as a mediator. Then take a second pass at your list, marking those you'd like to carry with you when you're marking. If you're having trouble getting started, try using my list from earlier in the chapter as a launching point.

Reflection Question 2.2
What are you truly passionate about when it comes to mediation and why?

For this question, consider only what you're most passionate about. Forget the rest for now. If you're not sure you feel any passion for mediation, use this opportunity to explore why that might be. We'll return to the work you begin in this question in a later chapter.

Reflection Question 2.3
What would happen if you replaced marketing tasks you dislike with a way of marketing that feels authentic and enjoyable?

The answer seems obvious at first, but I'm asking you to dig deeper. I'm asking you to really consider the replacement of tasks you dislike (and so probably don't do) with ones you enjoy. What would it *feel* like? How would it change the way you approach marketing?

CHAPTER 3

Creating Space for the Important

We often put off defining and achieving our goals because we fear that if we do not follow the 'way it is supposed to be done,' we will fail. Good news: The world in which we live today changes very quickly. New technologies, different sales venues, and amazing jobs are created every day. Therefore, the path to achieving an objective transforms daily, and, at times, hourly.—Romanus Wolter

To paraphrase Peter Drucker, effective people are not problem-minded; they're opportunity-minded. They feed opportunities and starve problems.—Stephen Covey

Stephen Covey, perhaps most widely known for the bestselling book, *The Seven Habits of Highly Effective People*, used to conduct a powerful demonstration in his speeches and workshops.

He'd show the audience a large glass jar, a pitcher of sand, and a bowl of rocks. The rocks represent the important work we need to do, the work that has the power to transform our lives and our practices. The sand represents the urgent matters we attend to day to day, like going to meetings, returning e-mail, and running errands.

He pours the sand into the large glass jar. There's a little bit of room left, so he tries to add the rocks. A few fit, but most don't. The glass jar, in that configuration, represents the way most of us navigate our days. The Important is hijacked by the Urgent.

He empties the large glass jar and begins again. This time, however, he adds the rocks first. Then he pours in the sand, which sifts into the nooks and crannies between the rocks. Everything fits, perhaps with a few grains of sand left over.

The glass jar, in the second configuration, is the image of an effectively mastered day: the Important gets first attention and there's still space for the Urgent. And, as you've no doubt experienced, the Urgent that doesn't fit probably wasn't urgent at all ... just filler.

If you're serious about building a thriving mediation practice, you must attend to the Important. It needs to be your priority, your commitment, and your driving force.

Here are reasons mediators have told me they can't fit practice development into their time:

- I'm a full-time attorney, and there's no extra space in my week.

- I work part-time outside the field and volunteer part-time at a community mediation center. There aren't enough hours in the week.

- I can't give up the income of a full-time job to market something I'm not sure is going to pay off.

- I'm barely keeping my head above water, what with raising kids, working, and going to school. When would I market?

- I've exhausted my savings trying to build this practice and can't invest more time or money until I've built up cash flow again.

Urgent feels safe because it's a familiar mode in a world that thinks it wants multitaskers. It feels good because crisis responders are valued.

Important feels risky, maybe even a bit unsafe, because it calls on you to dig deep, face your dream, and confront what you've been avoiding.

Your practice will not thrive if you fill your life with Urgent. How much of your day do you spend on the unimportant Urgent?

The Twenty Percent Rule

When I was in the initial stages of developing my private practice, I tapped the wise counsel of my local Small Business Development Center (SBDC), a division of the United States Small Business Administration. I'd managed large budgets as a college dean but had never put together financials for a small business. I'd chaired strategic planning committees but knew nothing about business plans. I was a self-starter but had never worked solo in a small business. The SBDC's services were free (and still are), and it was one of the best choices of my startup period.

The Burlington, Vermont, SBDC director (whose name I've forgotten or I'd attribute him enthusiastically) gave me two pieces of advice that still serve me today. I'll share one with you now and the second one in a later chapter. The first piece of advice he offered was this:

Plan to spend about 20 percent of your time on marketing activities.

Whoa, Nelly! That was certainly my initial reaction. But since I'd quit my powerful and well-paying job and certainly had time on my hands, I figure I had nothing to lose. It's still a general rule I use today.

It's easy enough to do when you're just starting out and have completely jumped ship like I did. But if you're juggling multiple professional identities and a life, then you're probably already dismissing the 20 Percent Rule as undoable.

Wait! Consider this question: 20 percent of *what* time? Your time on the earth? Your waking time? Your workweek?

Your 20 percent will be determined by two factors:

- How much you're able to commit to the Important instead of the safer and easier Urgent.

- How much Important time you can create in your week.

If you're just starting your business and don't have many clients yet, then you'll want to spend a significant portion of your time on marketing and other business development activities. Probably much more than twenty percent.

If you're a full-time attorney giving your life away to the law firm that hired you, you have some choices to make. You say you want to carve out an ADR practice, but are you committed to that dream, or is it idle thought to distract you with hope when you're burning the midnight oil?

Even 5 hours of freed time (out of a possible 168) for the Important can give you an hour of marketing. You can do a lot in an hour if you know what to do, have prepared yourself to do it, and want to do it. It's a place to start.

What would a 20 percent rule of thumb look like in your week? What would make it possible?

Make Marketing One of the Importants

If marketing hasn't traditionally caused you to leap from bed with the joy of anticipation each morning, here are some strategies for building business development time into your calendar without unduly draining other work that needs doing:

Strategy 1: Schedule time for marketing. Schedule dedicated marketing time into your calendar in the same way that you schedule time for other activities you consider important. Creating the space for business development activities helps ensure these actions won't get shoved to the wayside and allows you to focus and get depth. I aim for the equivalent of one day every one to two weeks. My ideal is a single full day, and I know others who commit to approximately 2 hours daily. The key is to find a rhythm that works for you.

Strategy 2: Make it sacred. It's tempting to reschedule marketing time, particularly if marketing activities haven't traditionally been enjoyable to you. Make the 20 percent commitment and stick to it for 90 days (or for as little as 21 days, if you choose a daily marketing routine), and it will become a habit for the long run.

Strategy 3: Make it a regular action. It's generally not helpful to avoid marketing for a while and then throw yourself into it for a long stretch of consecutive days. The most effective marketing approaches create continuity and momentum for yourself and regular connection with your target markets.

Strategy 4: Schedule "big thinking" retreats for yourself. If you've got a busy practice like mine or are transitioning from full-time work in another arena, then the opportunity for in-depth reflection about your craft and your business is hard to come by. For ten years I've scheduled quarterly "thinking retreats" of one to two days—and sometimes up to a week—and they have become such a treat that I look forward to them eagerly.

I do no other work or regular marketing activities during those periods. Instead, I use them to sit back and work my way through the bigger questions of my work: How am I doing? Is this direction working? What's not working? What do I want to do more/less of? Am I feeling stretched in a good way? I recommend choosing days when you won't be disturbed or tempted by other activities. I've even, on occasion, booked myself a room at a quiet inn in the mountains or on the coast ... someplace that I find inspiring and that feeds my soul. I have also occasionally met with a colleague for a two-day stretch, and we conducted a joint retreat, each focusing on our own ADR practice while also serving as a resource and sounding board for the other's reflection.

Strategy 5: Feed your mind. Some of my most successful marketing ideas come to me when I'm sitting in workshops, retreats, or gatherings I find intellectually titillating. Or when I'm doing creative activities (for me, this happens when I'm writing or dry stone wall building, two of my hobbies). Or when I chance upon a magazine article while sitting in an airport. Get out of your business and your ADR chair regularly. Renew and stimulate your mind, and you'll find the benefits go well beyond the creative activity or learning experience itself.

How can you make marketing one of the Importants?

But Business Is Hopping!

It's tempting to cut back on marketing when business is thriving. You may believe you don't have the time. Or maybe you conclude that the momentum has kicked in and now you can market less than before.

It could be.

But it's probably not.

The time to find out it's the latter isn't when you notice a slacking off in requests for information or in scheduled mediations, because by then, you've already lost some of the momentum you've been building.

Marketing is always a part of business ownership. If you choose to adopt the mind frame that it's part of what makes you a successful business owner, and toss out the mind frame that it's badly cooked spinach and that you've just got to force yourself through, you'll make the right choices for yourself.

How will you keep momentum going?

That Giant Sucking Sound

I can hear it sometimes. These days it's less frequent than it used to be, when I was a dean and practically the queen of urgent. When I stepped out of that role to devote myself full-time to mediation in the mid-1990s, my staff gave me a toy fire extinguisher as a remembrance of deaning days. It was a sadly apropos gift.

If you stop and listen carefully, you can hear it too.

It's the giant sucking sound of your day's Important work going down the drain when an Urgent item arrives on your doorstep. Sometimes the Urgent is the Important. But more often than not, it's simply that you've been hooked by an old habit.

I've said this is a book less about technique than frame of mind. If you agree with my premise, then you can probably understand that helpful habits of mind also apply to the way you navigate your day and make (or not make) space for building your ADR business.

Here are a few of my favorite strategies for keeping the Unimportant Urgent at bay while attending to the Important:

- **Batch E-mail and Telephone Calls:** There's nothing like a steady trickle of phone calls and e-mails to get in the way of concentration time. Multitasking schmultitasking. Multitasking is a fancy word for tending to the Urgent at the cost of the Important. I want to do something well when I do it. When I'm talking with or e-mailing clients and prospective clients, I want them to have my full attention, not the half of my brain that isn't still caught up in another task I was working on. When I'm working on business development, I likewise want to be able to offer that Important task my full attention. By batching e-mails and telephone calls as much as possible, I can achieve the full attention my clients, colleagues, and projects deserve.

- **E-mail Last Thing, Not First Thing:** I check my e-mail only three times daily: first thing, right before lunch, and just before closing up shop. It's important to note that my morning check is very focused, because checking e-mail in the morning is begging to hear that giant sucking sound. The morning check overlooks everything but business-related e-mails that need a response in the short term. There are some (see, for example, Tim Ferriss' book, *The 4-Hour Workweek*) who would even advocate skipping the first-thing-in-the-morning check entirely.

- **Set Goals Today for Tomorrow:** I jump-start my day by having thought about it the afternoon before. Before wrapping up each day, I set the next day's key goals and gather materials and information I'll need to dive right in. That way, I don't risk getting caught up in administrivia in the morning when I want to be working on the Important. I also prevent myself from whittling away at my Important time looking for files and other materials at the time I need them.

- **Emergency Access:** My clients know to call me if it's pressing, and I'll answer right then and there if it's possible. If it's not, I'll know they called and get back to them the minute I'm out of my mediation or other client session. That's because the clients I want to keep are Important.

The resulting workday has this general rhythm:

7:00 a.m. Power up the computer and place my day's two to three goals visibly in the space I'm working (my home office, my hotel room, my faculty space, etc.). Check e-mail and voicemail and deal only with those requiring my attention right now.

7:30 a.m. to 11:00 a.m. Important work that moves me toward my goals. Some of this is work with and for clients, and some of this is marketing, depending on the day. It's my best time of day, so the most important work is scheduled for this period.

11:00 a.m. Return calls I've missed during morning client sessions. Check e-mail for the second time that day and reply to everything that needs my attention. File or trash e-mails that are FYIs or require no action on my part.

12:00 p.m. Short lunch. I'm not a big lunch fan. Exceptions are lunches with prospective, current, and past clients. But I do take a break so that my brain and I get some sunlight.

12:30 p.m. to 3:00 p.m. Check on how I'm doing with my day's goals, then same as the 7:30–11:00 a.m. stretch. Maybe dance around my office a bit if it's a happy day and I've done well with my objectives.

3:00 p.m. Return calls and check e-mail again. Review tomorrow's schedule, set tomorrow's top goals, and gather all materials I need to launch smoothly into my day tomorrow.

4:00 p.m. Done. Unless I have a late client meeting, which happens occasionally.

These are rhythms that work well in my day, and I invite you to try them. Obviously, you'll want to gear them to your own schedule, since you may not rise at 4 a.m. like I do!

If your body clock is dramatically different, then also consider how to arrange your own workday rhythm to capitalize on your high-energy times.

What are your high-energy times? Do you capitalize on them?

Reflection Question 3.1
Is developing a thriving mediation practice truly important to you?

Why is developing a thriving mediation practice important to you? Spell out how you know it's one of the Importants.

Reflection Question 3.2
What's gotten in the way of making practice-building a priority for you?

Time for a look inside. It may be tempting to conclude that what's gotten in the way is lack of marketing know-how, or time. Go deeper, though. What's *really* gotten in your way?

Reflection Question 3.3
What habits will you toss?

What are the Unimportant Urgent or filler habits you have now that are getting in the way of the Important? List them and follow each with a short note about why you think it's a habit to toss.

Reflection Question 3.4
In order to create real space for what's important, what habits will you adopt?

Tossing out old habits isn't sufficient, because you'll create a void that the old habit will sneak in to fill when you're not looking. Don't give 'em the chance. Replace the old habits instead. List the new habits here and how you will employ them. The more specific your plan for employing the new habits, the better.

CHAPTER 4

Narrowing Your Market

In almost every market, the boring slot is filled. The product designed to appeal to the largest possible audience already exists, and displacing it is awfully difficult.—Seth Godin

It is said that if everyone is your customer, then no one is your customer.—Timothy Ferriss

When mediating, you understand the importance of knowing something about the stakeholders at the table. How you dress (Pin-striped suit? Birkenstocks?), the degree of formality you display, and even how you speak may be influenced by the environment in which you're mediating and the people you're serving.

Mediator Mindset Marketing taps into the same idea. Knowing to whom you're marketing influences what approaches you use, what outlets you choose for your marketing, the formality of your approach, and perhaps even the colors you choose for your business logo.

Not as Counterintuitive as it Seems

It may seem counterintuitive at first: A narrow target market creates stronger opportunity for business success than a broad one. And generalist mediation practices take longer to build than those serving very specific markets or those in specific niches.

For too many mediators, marketing becomes an effort to try to reach everyone who might have conflict and do a little bit of work in a variety of arenas, in the name of "keeping my options open."

However, choosing a narrow market yields far better results. Indeed, when I look at mediators who've been able to build thriving private practices in three to four years of effective practice building, they all began by cultivating specific markets.

A target market, by the way, is not the same as a market niche, though the two terms are sometimes used interchangeably. A target market is the group of people who you want as your clients. A market niche is the way you serve that market, through either the services you offer or the way you deliver those services.

What would happen if you realigned your thinking from "broad = safe" to "narrow = opportunity"?

How Narrow Target Markets Help Build Business

Narrow target markets work because with focus, you can speak with a clearer voice to the people you're trying to reach. When you try to write for or speak to everyone (in brochures, on your website, in speeches), you end up speaking to no one in particular, and your message gets watered down in your attempt to be all-inclusive.

They work because with a narrow target market, you know precisely how and where to find the people you're trying to reach. If, for example, you're targeting a rock musician market (I know of a mediator who does), you're probably going to find these folks in different places and through different venues than a mediator focusing on environmental disputes. When you know where to find the people you're trying to reach, you dramatically increase the return on your marketing investment. If you cast your net too widely, you spread yourself and your dollars very thin trying to reach everyone.

They work because you'll find it much easier to effectively engage people if you're truly interested in them. That's because you will convey greater energy when you pick a market in which you have a genuine interest—you won't be able to contain yourself, and you won't have to fake it. Similarly, you'll find it easier to engage people when you have invested time and energy in learning about them, because you will be able to speak with great clarity and insight directly to their specific types of conflict-related problems.

A single narrow target market is a place to begin, not the place you have to stay forever if you have diverse interests. When I founded my full-time practice in 1997, my single target market was higher education. At the time, I had worked in higher education for more than a decade, had served in both academic and senior leadership roles, and had served on think tanks and on professional association boards throughout the Northeast. I knew that audience and the issues they faced, and that audience knew me. I had lots of connections to gain access to key stake-holders, I could talk their language, and I felt at home on any campus. I loved being on a college campus and still feel like I'm "coming home" whenever I step onto one. Even in the rare occasions when I have to complete a marketing task that is mildly distasteful, knowing I am doing it for a market I love makes it far more palatable.

While I don't serve only higher education today, that work provided a strong foundation with a solid income from which to diversify later. While not every market will be the prime opportunity that higher education was a decade ago, I tell you this so that you understand clearly the ways that narrowing your focus can jump-start your success.

If you were to focus, for now, on a single target market, what opportunities come to mind?

The Target-Market Genie

Imagine for a moment that you could work with any client demographic you want. With the wave of a genie's hand, people in that demographic audience would be incredibly receptive to your ideas and offers of help.

But, as often seems the case with genies, there is a catch.

You must be able to describe your client demographic with at least seven very specific characteristics. That's because, the genie explains, not only is seven a lucky number, but his magic also only goes so far. He has to be able to *locate* the exact group you want in order to make your wish come true.

How would you describe that target demographic so that the genie could go and find them?

Four Market Selection Approaches

The first step in describing a genie-pleasing target market is to select markets that are prime for you and what you have to offer. I've found four ways to identify such markets and have used all four to great effect:

1. Markets in which you have strong interest

2. Markets that already know you (those in which you have experience or great contacts)

3. Markets that have a need you realize you can fill

4. Markets that find *you*, organically

The key is to pick one market, narrow it carefully, and define it clearly (more on this later). The target market you select may exist in only one of the above categories, or it may exist in several. I believe your target market should *always* include Category 1 (interest). If you're just starting out, your greatest leverage probably comes from target markets in Category 2 (experience, contacts). Categories 3 and 4 have the greatest promise for preventing "*Field of Dreams* marketing*," the trap of creating a service first and then hoping to find someone who wants it.

As you look through the four options, do any jump out at you as already developing?

Markets in Which You're Interested

As I noted above, choosing a market in which you have genuine interest enables you to approach your marketing work with enthusiasm and prevents you from having to fake passion where none exists. When you care deeply or are compelled by people, that interest will show. When you're ambivalent, you risk coming across as bland. People have good bull detectors.

Target markets in which you're interested are those that contain people in which you're interested, people who live or work in an arena that fascinates you, people with specific characteristics you admire, and so forth.

Questions to help you identify possible target markets in this category include:

- What kinds of people fascinate me?

- To what kinds of people am I often drawn?

- If I could hang out with a group of people I find compelling, what group would I join?

- When I was young, what professions were on my list of "What I want to be when I grow up"?

Markets in Which You're Experienced

If you're just starting out in the mediation field, it's a long haul to hang out a shingle in an arena where no one knows you. It's possible to create momentum in such an arena, but your timeline to produce steady income will be longer, and thus the capital you've set aside to keep you afloat will be need to be greater.

"Experienced" can be classified in a number of ways. Professionally experienced includes current and former careers. Academically experienced includes arenas associated with college majors or graduate degrees. Community service experienced includes volunteer posts or groups for which you've provided *pro bono* services. Vocationally experienced includes arenas in which you've been a loyal aficionado.

Questions to help you identify possible target markets in this category include:

- Is there an arena in which I have a lot of good contacts?

- In what markets am I already known, even if it's for different work?

- Outside of my prior work, in what arenas have I cultivated experience or contacts? (Consider your child's school system, for example, if you've been active there.)

Markets in Which There's a Need

One challenge the mediation field faces, which Mayer has pointed out and I discussed earlier in the book, is the notion that if we build it, they will come. But that hasn't happened. I will address a primary reason it hasn't happened in Chapter 6, but I will give you a brief preview now.

Creating a product or service and then seeking a market is a backward approach. From a business-building perspective, the likelihood of success is far greater when you notice an unfulfilled need, or an under-served market, or a twist on a well-catered need, and then develop your service or product.

A few years after starting my business, one of my higher education connections suggested I get in touch with a Boston-based environmental sustainability firm that was hiring. I wasn't job hunting, of course, but it looked like they had some needs I could fill, and I sat down with them to discuss how I might fill them as an independent contractor instead of as an employee. That association led to several years of personally fulfilling, professionally compelling consulting work in which I trained and coached campus environmental activists in using dialogue to further their "green" agendas.

It was some of the most enjoyable work I've ever done, and it took the least amount of effort to get it. The need was there first, I noticed it with the help of my friend, and the momentum carried me from there.

You can do it, too.

Questions to help you identify possible target markets in this category include:

- What groups, regions, or arenas could really benefit from the kind of skills I have?

- What social, political, cultural, or other trends suggest there could be need for problem-solving expertise like mine?

- What groups are hungry for better conflict resolution?

Markets that Come to You

About five years after I founded my mediation firm, I noticed a curious thing. I was getting a lot of links to my site and visits and notes from artists and graphic design professionals. This was not a market I had sought, nor was it one I would have guessed would come to me. But come to me they did.

I later discovered that a few well-respected voices in the arts world had mentioned my mediation firm at a gathering. These folks were influencers who'd had contact with me through my higher education work with several music and arts institutions in the United States. You just never know.

Sometimes, markets come to you. If you're not paying attention, you might miss them, because they're so unexpected. It may begin as a trickle, and if you're not attending to the sources for your referrals, inquiries, and Web site visits, you could fail to notice the trend.

So this is a market unlike those in the other categories, because you've simply got to be aware—and have good business systems to help you—in order to cultivate these markets.

Questions to help you identify possible target markets in this category include:

- Is my Web site getting traffic from any sources outside of the arenas I've targeted?

- Have referrals come my way from unexpected sources?

- What interest may have been expressed from groups I didn't expect and therefore didn't notice?

Sneezers, Connectors, and Transformers

For every market, there are influencers. Some of those influencers are people outside your target market but who hold the respect or attention of people in your market. And, preferably, some of those influencers are people already in your target market.

Your most effective marketing will include efforts to reach influencers, since they help you leverage your efforts.

Marketing pro Seth Godin calls such influencers Sneezers, the people who can spread the good word about what you offer just as a virus can be spread by a sneeze. Diffusion of Innovation and sustainability maven Alan AtKisson calls them Change Agents and Transformers, because they play key roles in promoting new ideas and are the early adopters, respectively. *Tipping Point* author Malcolm Gladwell calls them Connectors:

> What makes someone a Connector? The first—and most obvious—criterion is that Connectors know lots of people. They are the kinds of people who know everyone … Connectors are important for more than simply the number of people they know. Their importance is also a function of the kinds of people they know.

Who are your target market's Sneezers, Connectors, and Transformers? How can you connect with them?

The Credibility Factor

This is a good time to mention professional credibility again.

Good credibility and success with mediation marketing go hand-in-hand, because once you've attracted a market's interest, the degree to which you can deliver on your promises will determine not only if they select you for the help they need, but also the likelihood of referring others to you after they have seen you in action.

Credibility is based, in part, on how good you are at what you do. I've already discussed the value of being a good mediator and won't repeat those ideas.

But I do want to contrast that with a trend toward "fake it until you make it" credibility. Folks who buy into that way of thinking believe that if you study a bit and learn to replicate the language of leading thinkers and writers in a field, you can catch up on the experience front once the clients start coming in. Those who think that way believe that as long as you know just a bit more than your clients, then that's good enough.

Just the other day, a friend told me of running into an attorney who'd hired a mediator whose marketing skill was excellent but who had minimal training and below-average experience in the specialized technical arena to which he marketed. The attorney told my friend, "That was the worst mediation I'd ever seen. He couldn't understand anything we were discussing, and we ended up paying *him* while we educated him. I was embarrassed for the mediator. I'll never hire him again." Not only wouldn't he hire that mediator again, he was clearly comfortable telling others about the negative experience.

Be credible. Don't overpromise, because the hype catches up with and then fries you. I'm not talking about stretching yourself slightly in order to continue your professional development. I'm talking about stretching yourself beyond your capacity and in way that serves clients poorly.

In what ways are you most credible to your market? In what ways are you not?

Reflective Question 4.1
Who will be your primary narrow target market?

This is where the pedal hits the metal. Pick a single, narrow market using one of the four targeting approaches described above. The rest of this book assumes you've selected one, committed to it, and are ready to begin cultivating it. Even if you're not sure it's the right market to choose at this time, pick one to focus on in the remaining pages ... future questions will help you determine if it's a market that's an effective choice for you.

Reflective Question 4.2
Can you describe your target market in enough detail that they're findable?

Remember the genie's one condition? You need to be able to describe your target market in sufficient enough detail that the genie can actually *locate* them. The genie suggested you be able to describe them with at least seven identifying characteristics. Answer more if you can (the more the better) and be sure you can answer the first one in detail. If you can't answer enough of the questions, it's a signal that you may still be thinking too broadly about your market. Narrow it further.

- Where, online or in the physical world, can they be found (*e.g.*, Wal-Mart, gardening chat rooms, the library, family court)? In other words, where to do they congregate or hang out?

- Where do they live and/or work?

- What do they do for a living?

- What interests do they have?

- What do they spend money on?

- What do they do with their spare time?

- What problems do they face? (Think beyond just conflict-related problems.)

- What is their biggest conflict-related problem?

- What services and products do they buy? (Think beyond conflict-related services.)

- What are their primary racial, ethnic, economic, political, cultural, and social characteristics?

- What do they value most? Least?

- How old are they?

CHAPTER 5

Uncovering Interests

Your interests are intangible motivations that lead you to take [a] position—your needs, desires, concerns, fears, and aspirations.— William Ury

Interest-based bargainers believe that settlements in negotiations are reached because a party has succeeded in having his or her interests satisfied ... They are of three broad types: substantive, procedural, and psychological.—Christopher Moore

If you approach disputes from an interest-based orientation, then you're already seasoned in working with interests from the mediator's chair. This chapter invites you to extend your application of interest-based work into the marketing realm.

An old trap for business owners is to promote products and services based on the features they offer. Marketing experts challenge us to speak not from a features orientation but from a benefits orientation.

I'm challenging you to extend your thinking further ... from benefits to interests.

Are You Selling a Shovel?

There's an old marketing story about selling shovels.

Some marketers sell shovels by focusing on *features*: The strength of the shovel, the comfort of the grip, the weight of the item, the durability of the materials, the beauty of the design.

More savvy marketers sell shovels by focusing on the *benefits* the shovel offers: They focus on the holes buyers want to dig, not the shovel itself. They focus on ease of use, effects of good ergonomics, digging speed, ability of the shovel's sharp edge to cut through small roots, and so on.

Mediation mind frame marketers focus on the *interests* people want met by the hole and the shovel: More relaxation time. Less blood, sweat, and tears. Stronger fences to keep beloved pets safe. No back pain. Less worry.

When you market your mediation services, are you selling shovels, holes, or relaxation time?

Features, Benefits, and Interests

From a scan of one hundred mediator Web sites, it appears many, if not most, mediators are selling shovels.

If you're in this group, you're trying to sell mediation's features as a way to convince your market to buy. Features-based mediation marketing looks like these items I pulled randomly from ADR websites:

1. Mediation allows you to reach mutually agreeable solutions.

2. We encourage parties to look to the future instead of the past.

3. Mediation is quicker and less expensive than litigation.

4. It produces agreements that are based on the principles of fairness.

5. It's private and confidential.

6. You'll benefit from having an impartial third party helping you.

7. Mediation has a high rate of compliance with agreement.

8. Mediated agreements often stand the test of time.

With or without the mind-numbing jargon, these items tell the prospective buyer virtually nothing about how mediation really helps them. They're written from the perspective of the mediator, not from the perspective of someone who's asking, "What's in it for me?"

Entrepreneur.com explains why the features-based approach is so common:

> Most SOHO [Small Office Home Office] owners decide what business to start based on two factors: 1) what they're good at and like to do, and 2) what they assume possible customers will buy. Often those latter assumptions are correct, but small-business marketers also assume that prospects will understand why they should buy the product or service just because they've been told about it. Thus, business owners only communicate the features of their product or service to prospective customers and neglect to mention the benefits ... When you try to sell the features of your product or service, you're making the customer do all the work to figure out why they want the feature. It's in a seller's best interest to draw the connection for them.

So if features-based marketing loses the message in translation, what about benefits-based marketing? Based on the above list, benefits-based mediation marketing might look like this:

1. You retain control over what happens and any solutions.

2. You won't have to stay trapped in the past.

3. You'll save money and time.

4. You'll achieve fair and just results.

5. Mediation will help keep problems from leaking out.

6. The person helping you won't take sides or sit in judgment of you.

7. Mediation increases the likelihood that everyone will follow through on the agreement.

8. Mediation helps you achieve solutions for the long term.

Better. Definitely better. The prospective client asking "What in it for me?" (WIIFM) gets pretty close to an answer with the second list.

But I think we can do even better, using a principle you may already use when you're sitting in the mediator's chair: Interests. Using the same list, interest-based marketing might look like this:

1. Freedom of choice; autonomy.

2. Freedom to move on with your life.

3. Have resources to use in ways you really want; strengthen your business bottom line.

4. Being treated fairly; achieving justice.

5. Maintaining your privacy.

6. Preventing others' harsh judgment.

7. Being treated fairly and equitably.

8. Not having to spend future time still dealing with the same problem.

If you were to turn to a mediator right now for an unresolved conflict in your own life, how would you answer the question, "What's in it for me?"

Uncover Your Market's Key Interests

Once you know your target market, you can begin to identify key interests that are being thwarted by the problems they face. (I'll say more about identifying those problems in Chapter 6.)

One theory behind interest-based bargaining is that parties to a conflict are more likely to agree to a solution that meets one or more of their most important interests. The thinking is the same for your market: *They're more likely to agree to a service that helps them meet one or more of their most important interests.*

If you're familiar with uncovering interests from the mediator's chair, then you know that some of the best questions to ask get at the "why" behind the position. Building on that approach, here are some questions you might ask yourself or members of your market to uncover interests:

- What are your most pressing problems getting in the way of?

- Why do you care about your pressing problems getting addressed?

- What will relief or resolution of those pressing problems allow you to do or accomplish?

- If those pressing problems didn't exist, what could you achieve?

What Kinds of Interests?

In the quotation used at the beginning of this chapter, Christopher Moore identified three common categories of interest: substantive, procedural, and psychological.

As you begin to identify your market's key interests, I invite you to keep all three categories in mind. Moore can offer us some further insight about how these interests differ from one another:

> Substantive interests refer to the needs that an individual has for particular goods such as money and time. Substantive interests are often the central needs on which negotiations focus.
>
> Procedural interests refer to the preferences that a negotiator has for the way that the parties discuss their differences and the manner in which the bargaining outcome is implemented ...
>
> Psychological interests refer to the emotional and relationship needs of the negotiator, both during and as a result of the negotiations.

What kinds of interests do members of your target market have? How can you propose to address those interests through your services?

Reflective Question 5.1
What are your target market's most important interests?

What interests do members of your target market have with respect to the problems they most commonly face? Of those interests, what are the most important ones they'd be willing to invest time and money into getting met? If you're not sure you've found interests important enough, ask ten to twenty members of your target market for their feedback. Just like in mediation, it's better to ask and confirm than only guess at interests.

Reflective Question 5.2
What will speak compellingly to your market's key interests?

Forget what others have written about the ways mediation and ADR serve the public. Forget the standard answers to the questions, "How does mediation help?" or "Why choose mediation?" or "What are the benefits of mediation?"

Instead, put yourself in the heart, mind, and shoes of an ideal member of your target market. If you've done all the exercises so far, you're starting to know them pretty well. Stand in their shoes, feel the pain they experience from their most pressing problems, feel the hope they have of their key interests getting met, and then answer this question: What can I tell them about my services that will speak directly to their interests?

Experiment with sample answers, both written and verbal.

CHAPTER 6

Reframing How You Help

The way to change the game is to change the frame.—William Ury

The art of reframing is to maintain the conflict in all its richness but to help people look at it in a more open-minded and hopeful way.—Bernard Mayer

You know this as a mediator: The way parties frame the problem they're trying to solve can have tremendous impact on the outcome of their conversation. Truly effective frames can change the way people understand the problem they're trying to address, influence the path taken to solving it, and make visible solutions that may have been unnoticed before.

Mediators understand the art of problem framing. Effective frames, whether generated by the parties, by the mediator, or through the joint effort of all involved, help reconceptualize a problem and make it more understandable, manageable, or solvable.

Just as you help disputing parties reconceptualize the problems they face, this chapter invites you to take what you know about framing and apply it to marketing in two essential ways:

- Reframe *what* you do.

- Reframe *how you talk about* what you do.

Being of Service

At a graduation ceremony for Woodbury College (where I teach mediation), a newly minted master's graduate was one of the speakers. In preparation for her speech, Mary Ellen Otis had asked her fellow students what they had planned to do with their conflict management and dispute resolution skills at the time they enrolled. Many of them wanted to be Mediators in the traditional sense of the term, or ombudsmen, or consultants. She then asked them what they planned to do with their skills now that they were completing the master's journey.

She summed up their second set of responses with the simple words of one of her fellow students: *Be of service.*

At the start of a term, I often ask my new graduate students why they want to be mediators. I ask participants in mediation trainings a similar question: Why are you here? The most common responses would sound familiar to most of you reading this book:

- To help people find a more peaceful resolution of their conflicts.

- To reduce the damage caused by poorly managed conflict.

- To help people choose a less debris-filled way to differ.

- To help people the way I was helped during my divorce.

- To create healthy dialogue in families and family-owned businesses.

- To help build peace in the world, one dispute at a time.

Why are *you* here?

What if There Were No More Labels?

Imagine this: You wake up, switch on your favorite morning news program as you get ready for work, and learn that as of today, all people are outlawed from labeling their work. There are no more reference librarians, dog behaviorists, or computer sales associates. Instead, when asked, "what do you do?" people everywhere on the planet may only describe how they serve others, without jargon or traditional labels of any kind.

As of today, there are now only people who help people locate materials to support their research, assist dogs in channeling their energy in constructive ways, or guide people in selecting the best computer technology for their individual needs.

So of course, there are no more Mediators and there is no more Mediation. And when people ask what you do, you can no longer reply with, "I'm a mediator."

What would you replacement answer be?

Being a Mediative Influence

There are lots of reasons we choose to be mediators, and most of them have little to do with the formal process we call Mediation. I offered a few of them at the beginning of the chapter, and you may have many additions to my sample list.

In the introduction I explained that my choice of the term "mediator" in this book is meant to convey not the formal Mediation process role, but "one who serves as a mediative influence."

My intention in using this concept is to invite you to expand your thinking, if you haven't already, beyond Mediation. If you already offer assistance through a variety of roles in addition to Mediator, then this is not new thinking for you. If you have primarily committed yourself to being a Mediator in the formal sense, then I suggest that your business success—and perhaps the future of the dispute resolution field—will depend on the degree to which you and other mediators can expand your thinking.

When you reframe what you do from "Mediator" to "mediative influence," you open yourself to ways of serving your market that may have been invisible to you before now. You open yourself to a two-way conversation with your market because you're no longer trying to educate them about or persuade them to try only the formal process called Mediation.

It's hard to persuade people to buy when the service you're offering isn't necessarily the right fit for their needs. This is the bind the field of Mediation has gotten itself into.

How can you reframe your way of being in this field?

Beginner's Mind

Another way to open yourself to an expanded view for serving your market is by adopting a Beginner's Mind. The Zen concept of Beginner's Mind describes a state in which a person can work with many possibilities and avoid getting stuck on any single path or approach. As described by Suzuki in *Zen Mind, Beginner's Mind*, "the most important thing is not to be dualistic ... This does not mean a closed mind, but actually an empty mind and a ready mind. If your mind is empty, it is always ready for anything; it is open to everything. In the beginner's mind there are many possibilities; in the expert's mind there are few."

When you approach the ideas of service and roles using Beginner's Mind, you orient yourself not to your present expertise but to a wider way of understanding what you offer. A list of wider ways a mediator could serve clients might include:

- Strategist
- Advocate
- Conflict management educator
- Coach
- Mediator
- Facilitator
- Ombudsman
- Negotiator
- Consultant or advisor

This is by no means an exhaustive list and is intended primarily to whet your curiosity and thinking, especially if you haven't before considered alternative roles to Mediator.

If you were to take off your expert's hat (I know, I know, the glue is very well set), what would you do in order to adopt a Beginner's Mind?

Talking to Your Market

In the introduction, I discussed Bernard Mayer's concerns, as expressed in his book *Beyond Neutrality*, that our field has been overreliant on the ideas of resolution and neutrality.

When you stop thinking of yourself solely as a Mediator and start thinking of yourself as a mediative influence, you begin to address this problem front and center. As the earlier list suggests, being a mediative influence may mean assuming roles that are neither neutral nor aimed solely at resolution.

How do you decide what roles and services are right for you and of interest to your chosen target market?

You ask them.

The work you did in Chapter 4 helped you identify a narrow target market that is locatable, so you know whom you're trying to serve and exactly where to find them.

Some of your most important market research is to find out what they want, why they want it (their interests!), and where there's a confluence with your own passions and skills. In the next chapter I'll discuss in greater detail how to engage your target market in such a dialogue. For now, though, begin experimenting with a way of being, a mind frame, that's less "Mediator," and more a "mediative influence."

What does *your* market want from a mediator?

The Problems They Most Want Solved

People, families, groups, and communities have problems that range from those barely on the radar screen to those that scream for attention. The services you offer and the way you talk about those services must focus on the problems that fall somewhere in that latter half of an individual's or group's problem continuum, as they are more likely to receive attention and get addressed.

To discover and learn about those problems, you'll need to be familiar with the work and/or home lives of those you're trying to reach. Having a clearly defined narrow target market makes this task easier, since you know where to find them in order to gather this kind of information.

If you know your target market well, then you already have some insight into their most pressing problems. Beware of assuming you already know the answer (a version of the Expert's Dilemma, which I will discuss in a moment). Instead, talk directly to some members of your market to gather additional information.

If you don't yet know your target market in-depth, the best place to begin is by asking members of that target market. You want to be sure that they have pressing problems that 1) need your help and 2) are important enough that they'd invest time and money in solving them. If you discover through your research that this is not the case, you will want to rethink your chosen target market before further developing your marketing strategy. Conducting this research, then, is absolutely critical to your success.

For example, one mediator who prefers to work primarily with families and with parent-teen conflicts gathered ideas based on her own experience as a parent and from both casual and formal conversations with other parents and influencers in her market. After several weeks of conversations and making quick reminder notes, she identified the following problems as standing out most for members of her target market in the geographic region she serves:

- Ugly interchanges between parents and teens at home, leaving everyone feeling like they're walking on eggshells.

- Parents who feel alienated from their teens and helpless to change the dynamic at home or school.

- Teens who are in pain and feel the adults in their lives can't help.

- Substance abuse, eating disorders, and other ways teens attempt to salve their pain.

- Petty crime, runaways, school delinquency, and dropping grades.

- Parents losing time at work, and therefore income, in order to deal with their teens' problems at school and in the community.

- Teens caught between divorcing or already divorced parents who continue to play out their divorce grievances daily.

What problems do your target markets most want solved?

The Expert's Dilemma

When you're familiar with a role or passionate about a certain process (like Mediation), then it's easy to get caught in what I call the Expert's Dilemma.

The Expert's Dilemma happens when you try to describe a concept about which you're an expert to someone who is not an expert. You understand they are not an expert and may not have the same complex grasp of the topic as you do, yet you don't want to reduce the concept to simplistic terms because you know simplistic will not suffice. You struggle to convey the topic in all its complex glory yet in terms the uninitiated can, as a colleague of mine says, "grock it" (*i.e.*, really grasp it).

The result of the Expert's Dilemma in mediation marketing is often either a watered-down set of vague promises ("I help people identify mutually agreeable solutions to complex problems") or a jargon-filled statement ("I serve as an impartial third party who helps people negotiate their disputes in such a way that key interests are met and acted upon.")

One way to outsmart Expert's Dilemma is to break your thinking into discrete parts and distill your language to the simplest (not the most simplistic) terms possible. I call it a Role Reframe.

Before I introduce you to the Role Reframe, consider this: If you could turn to the person next to you in the bus and describe your offer in a way that would leave them singing in the aisles, what would you say?

Reframing the Way You Talk about Yourself

Picture yourself at party, networking social, or other event where someone sidles up and asks, "So what do you do for a living?"

Do you answer, "I'm a mediator"? Or, "I do ADR work"?

As I was preparing to write this chapter, I decided to experiment with the first answer in order to better understand people's responses to it. Over several weeks, I used that simple reply in a number of gatherings, and the reactions generally sorted into these categories:

- **Intrigue.** Interest in any compelling stories I might have about the folks I've served (worry not, I don't share).

- **Assumptions.** That I must be an attorney. That I must be an arbitrator. That I must work with unions. That I must be a divorce mediator.

- **Wrinkled noses.** The "Ew" reaction, as though I must be a bit addled or voyeuristic, followed by my conversation partner moving quickly on to someone else.

- **Curiosity.** Curious about how I got into it, what mediation is, or how I find clients.

- **Me too.** The "oh, I mediate all the time at home" reaction. Or at work. Or for friends.

Some of these reactions are worth preventing. Some, if time permitted, could evolve into an engaging conversation that might yield some leads.

But almost all of them had a missing ingredient.

A key ingredient.

And therefore, a missed opportunity.

They failed to create a connection between the other person's own interests and what I offer. Instead, they almost universally turned the conversation back to *me*, or to a vague person out there who might need a mediator.

While it might feel good to talk about ourselves and how we got into the work, it's an error to assume the person we're speaking with will translate that back into how we might serve *them*. And while it may seem useful to speak about the people "out there somewhere" who use mediators, it's also an error to assume the person we're speaking with will translate that back into ways we might serve their own needs.

We want to reframe how we talk about ourselves so that we don't have to rely on the hope of a good translation.

Do you need a translator when you answer the question, "What do you do?"

Create Your Role Reframe

Your Role Reframe offers a new and compelling answer to the "what do you do?" question. It has three parts:

Role Reframe Part 1: Your ten-word description. This is a brief overview of the way you are of service to others and includes information about whom you serve. The language is jargon-free, tight, and understandable to your target audience. It isn't worrisome if not everyone understands what you offer, as long as those in your target market(s) do, so draft your description with them in mind.

Role Reframe Part 2: The ways you deliver. You can name the ways you deliver on what you described in Part 1 as either a role or a service.

Role Reframe Part 3: Your "for instance" question. The last part of your response is a question that invites your listener into a brief exchange. It ties what you said in your Part 1 and Part 2 to them in order to create context and meaning about what you said. In essence, it's the way you segue into helping your listener translate what you do into their reality. It turns the conversation back to them for the beginning of what could become real dialogue.

For example, the family mediator I referenced earlier crafted the following key phrases to best describe the work she most wants to do:

- Teach people how to approach conflict so it doesn't inflict damage.

- Help people learn basic negotiation and communication skills for defusing tense family situations.

- Assist people in figuring out how to be more fully heard.

- Help families work through difficult conversations together.

She then considered those descriptions and identified the following as roles she wants to take on in her work:

- Trainer

- Mediator

- Parenting mentor and coach

And finally, after multiple drafts and trying phrases out with parents and teens she knows, she crafted this Role Reframe:

I help families use conflict to strengthen their relationships instead of creating divides. I do this as a mediator, helping families talk out their differences.

I also do this as a trainer, teaching parents how to handle disputes better. And I do this as a parenting mentor, working one-on-one with parents who want to communicate more effectively with their teen and pre-teen children. For instance, have you ever run into a difficult situation with one of your children, or know someone who has?

When asked what they do for a living, many people answer the question and stop there. They label themselves ("I'm a mediator") or, if they're savvy, they offer their own version of a Role Reframe. But then they stop, leaving the listener to react … or not react.

Your "for instance" question is critical, because it's what turns your words from a reply into an offering of conversation. It's what enables you to begin building a connection between what you do and what the listener (or the friend, family member, neighbor, or co-worker of the listener) might need. It's what turns the conversation back to a focus on the listener, instead of on you or the Unnamed Person Out There.

Try it out loud. Answer in a new way. What do you do?

Comfortable but Not Rehearsed

I invite you to make your Role Reframe comfortable sounding without seeming rehearsed, rote, or memorized. A memorized answer is simply applying technique. Being comfortable is adopting a way of thinking about your work and how you explain it in a way that extends conversation effectively.

I invite you to draft your own Role Reframe (there's an exercise in the next section) and then work on it until you can speak about it naturally and genuinely. Instead of memorizing your response, consider memorizing the three sections of a Role Reframe ... your response will then come freshly each time your reply.

There are two other versions of a Role Reframe approach that I discovered while researching others who've developed an idea like the one I've used for years. If the way I've presented it here isn't quite clicking for you, then I recommend the Romanus Wolter and Michael Port books listed in the References section in the back of the book.

When you're talking with trusted friends, how do you talk about what you do? What would happen if you said the same things to prospective clients?

Reflective Question 6.1
How can you best be of service?

Take time to reflect deeply on the following questions. Begin by writing for 5 minutes on each question and resist the temptation to move to the next question before that period is up. Instead, allow space for your answers to percolate and keep writing, even if the initial responses aren't fully formed.

- Why are you (or why do you want to be) a mediator or Mediator?

- In what ways are you trying to be of service to people in conflict?

- What is it that you're tying to help people achieve through Mediation?

- What problem does mediation solve for people?

Once you believe you've thoroughly answered each question, review your responses and select three to four ways you're trying to be of service that are the most meaningful or energizing for you

Reflective Question 6.2
How can you be a mediative influence?

If you were to cease wearing the label "Mediator" and instead wear the role of "mediative influence," what would that mean for how you are of service? What would it take for you to shift or add to your role repertoire?

Reflective Question 6.3
What are your target market's ten most pressing problems?

If you're already very familiar with your target market because you've worked in or with that arena, you should be able to complete this exercise now. If the target market you've chosen is a new one to you, then you may need to gather more information from that market before you can complete this exercise.

Identify the top ten problems your target market faces daily or regularly. Don't worry initially whether or not those problems are associated with conflict. Instead, focus on the problems that cause the most pain and are the most omni-present in their day-to-day work or home lives. After you've identified them, then you can analyze ways that ADR may or may not help.

Reflective Question 6.4
What is your Role Reframe?

Using the "Create Your Role Reframe" section as a guide, as well as the example provided there, craft your Role Reframe. You will probably go through several drafts of this until you've honed it to a satisfactory degree. Remember to keep the jargon to a minimum and aim for conciseness. They don't call it an Elevator Pitch for nothing!

CHAPTER 7

Building Dialogue with Your Market

In [Martin] Buber's philosophy, life itself is a form of meeting and dialogue is the "ridge" on which we meet. In dialogue, we penetrate behind the polite superficialities and defenses in which we habitually armor ourselves. We listen and respond to one another with an authenticity that forges a bond between us.—Daniel Yankelovich

When I first began developing my own successful marketing mind frame, dialogue was the cornerstone of it. I said to my husband, "I don't want to talk *at* my market. People are sick to death of being talked at ... that's exactly the experience of my clients, too. People want to be talked *with*."

I knew I'd be able to get jazzed about marketing if I could figure out mechanisms to talk with my market and engage them in dialogue, an act I already valued and understood. It seemed the most natural thing in the world to take what all good mediators know about dialogue and extend its use.

Apparently, folks who weren't mediators were thinking the same, though I wasn't aware of it at the time.

I don't know who first proposed the idea of dialogue marketing or conversational marketing, but I first stumbled on its use outside of my own private approach when I read *The Cluetrain Manifesto*. The book helped me realize that I wasn't alone in approaching marketing this way. Maybe it's why I'd had so much success so early in my ADR practice's life.

In this chapter, I'll offer you some of the same groundwork I've used and taught others to use in building dialogue with their market, both on the Internet and in person.

Fair Warning

This isn't a chapter about blogging or e-zines or podcasting or video blogging.

I'll mention them, yes, but I'm not going to waste your time telling you how to do any of them. There are plenty of resources that do that, including several at MakingMediationYourDayJob.com.

I'm not going to review that material here, because there's something else you need to do first: figure out how to transfer your mediator knowledge about dialogue into actually building dialogue with your market.

Then you'll know what tools to buy and use.

Daylight in a Beautiful Garden

Imagine that you're in a beautiful garden. The temperature is perfect, and the sun is shining. Fragrant blossoms surround you (if you have hay fever, there are no symptoms in this magic world I'm creating for you), and birds sing lightly in the background. The garden is large and airy yet walled in to create privacy. Flowering vines cover the ten-foot-high, stone walls. All your needs are taken care of, including your favorite foods and comfy lounge chairs, pillows, and hand-quilted throws for snoozing and relaxing.

Now imagine that you have the incredible opportunity to spend two days in this garden with a single person who is an absolutely perfect match for your ideal client in your target market. You have the good fortune of knowing, in advance, that you'll be in the garden for two days, so you have some planning time. You're charged with emerging from the garden having marketed your services successfully to that person. But you may not sell, convince, or persuade in any way. You may only engage them in an act of dialogue.

How would you use your time to build real dialogue with this person?

Mediators Already Know

What do good mediators already know about dialogue and its value?

We know a lot. As professions go, ours is one of the leaders to tap into the power of dialogue. We know, for example, that:

Genuine dialogue increases understanding. Because real dialogue is, in part, a learning conversation, dialogue creates opportunity for new information to surface and be considered thoughtfully. Participants in a dialogue are encouraged to question and to bring their genuine curiosity to the table. Dialogue is generative.

When considered through a marketing lens, we can easily see how dialogue increases our market's understanding of what we offer and our understanding of what our market most needs and wants.

Genuine dialogue helps build a relationship. Because dialogue gets people actively involved, it creates engagement. Authentic engagement sows the seeds of trust over time, particularly when dialogue becomes the communications norm in the relationship. Dialogue is invigorating and involving and creates real human connection.

In marketing, dialogue helps build a relationship between you and members of your target market. A relationship creates opportunity for prospective clients to sample you and to learn more about how you can serve them. It gives you the opportunity to get to know them better … and so serve them better.

Genuine dialogue leads to more informed decision-making. Some goals of dialogue can be to solve problems and jointly reflect on options and opportunities. The best dialogue leads to ownership and buy-in because it's the result of each person's full and voluntary participation. As participants in a dialogue consider a problem or idea from multiple perspectives, new options are made visible.

Dialogue in marketing helps your market make informed decisions about purchasing services from you because you've helped educate them in your marketing conversations. And it helps you make more informed decisions about what you offer to your market.

Genuine dialogue isn't hype. It's not manipulative, and it's not put on for the sake of an unspoken motive. It's candid and honest, and it draws on what's best in you. According to technology innovator and conversation marketing expert Shel Israel,

> People respond better to lowered voices spoken in credible tones than they do to the aggressive in-your-face marketing speak as is evidenced in everything from TV ads to the pap-lingo of so many websites. If common sense prevailed, marketers would understand that simply conversing with custom-

ers, prospects, partners, investors and employees is more effective. People listen better and longer when you just talk to them and listen back. All too often professional marketers lose their credibility by hyperbole, hubris and amplification.

How can you market with a lowered voice spoken in credible tones?

Marketing as Dialogue: You Already Know How

Some of your most tried and true mediator tools also serve as your best dialogue marketing tools.

Your curiosity. The frame of mind with which you enter a conversation helps determine whether or not that conversation reaches the level of true dialogue. As you know from mediating, entering a conversation in order to persuade, manipulate, or strong-arm will only get you so far. Such conversations are a trading of assumptions, judgments, diagnoses, and positional debates that differ from dialogue. Building dialogue comes from a genuine interest, a willingness to try ideas on for size, a curiosity or learning mindset, and a willingness to uncover assumptions that are derailing effective outcomes.

Artful inquiry. The ability to ask useful questions at the right time and with the right language to convey them is a mediator's stock in trade. When you ask your good curiosity-based questions (as opposed to leading questions, which are akin to outdated manipulation marketing), you open new avenues of conversation with your market. Good questions lead to good learning.

Deep listening. Distilling and reflecting what you've heard helps you check your own understanding, helps the speaker clarify their own thinking and feeling, and helps others understand the speaker's perspective more effectively than they may have otherwise. In partnership with artful inquiry, attentive and deep listening to your market's responses allows you to craft services that best meet their needs and identify ways to talk about those services that will attract their attention in return.

Permission to change. When you do all of the above, you put your assumptions at risk. You may learn that your market wants something different than what you presently offer. Or you may learn that what they want is what you offer, but they don't understand you yet. Your most effective dialogue marketing creates space for you to take in new information and change what you do or how you talk about it.

What else do you know about building dialogue? How can you use it to generate dialogue with your market?

A Paradigm Shift

When I began my quest to find a way to enjoy marketing and make it more effective for me than I suspected traditional techniques would be, I did what I had been trained to do both as an educator and as a mediator: I set out to learn.

I didn't know then what I know now, that I had stumbled onto something that really worked, felt authentic and honest, and created instant connection with prospective clients. When I approached my market with a desire to learn, I allowed my natural curiosity to inform the way our conversations unfolded.

Instead of "Let me tell you about how mediation helps," I asked, "When you're in a conflict situation, what do you most need?"

Instead of "Mediation is a terrific way to craft mutually satisfying resolutions to problems," I asked, "Would you ever hire a mediator to help? Why or why not?"

And instead of "I'd love to talk to you more about ways I can serve your organization," I asked, "If you had access to someone who had studied conflict and how it unfolds, what do you think you'd most want to know from them?"

Instead of feeling like I was shamelessly self-promoting in a way that felt and looked slick, I entered and emerged from these conversations with the enthusiasm of Sherlock Holmes on the trail of something important. I discovered that my genuine interest and curiosity, coupled with a letting go of the need to sell, hooked my conversation partners in ways that traditional marketing approaches would not. They wanted to talk, they wanted to reflect, and their own curiosity was piqued.

If you were to shift from a selling conversation to a dialogue with your market, what do you think could happen?

Indulge in Learning Conversations

What is the problem you're trying to solve with your marketing efforts? Here are some typical answers:

- Convince people to give ADR a try.

- Get more comfortable with selling.

- Learn to like schmoozing.

- Educate the public about the benefits of mediation.

- Figure out how to afford advertising without selling the farm.

- Figure out how to sell intangible services that have no guarantee of success.

- Figure out how to get people to want what I have to offer.

- Get more business!

Most of us traditionally associate marketing with self-promotion, convincing someone to buy what we're offering, and maybe educating people about alternative dispute resolution. I suspect I'm not alone in feeling alienated by this approach ... I don't like it used on me, so I don't want to use it on someone else.

Would you enjoy marketing more if your primary aim isn't selling and self-promotion? I'm betting most of you would say yes. The truth is that traditional "sales-y" marketing approaches are fast going the way of the dinosaur. An increasingly skeptical public has become jaded about and resilient toward traditional advertising and mainstream media. The onslaught of ads is beginning to deafen us to their messages. While marketing and advertising are not the same, many associate them with each other because they've been bedfellows.

When we reframe marketing as dialogue or as a learning conversation, then we naturally bring a new curiosity to the task. Instead of persuading, convincing, and wrangling, we can't help but want to know:

- What do people in conflict *really* need and want?

- Why aren't people buying?

- What other ways I can use my particular skill set in conflict situations?

- Who are the people I'm best situated to help?

You're still in that garden … what do you want to ask the person who's with you? What questions could they answer that would help you know how best to serve and talk about the ways you serve?

In-Person Dialogue

If dialogue is, at its most basic level, a two-way conversation, then your best marketing efforts would include opportunities for such an exchange to take place, a chance for conversation to begin. Some will never go further, but some will blossom into real conversation, real interest, and real dialogue.

There are many opportunities to build in-person dialogue opportunities with your target market, and you know about most of them: networking events; in-person meetings; speeches to civic groups, and opportunities to chat with audience members. While these types of events turn off some mediators, you may find them far less painful if you approach them with a "building dialogue" plan instead of "selling my services" orientation.

Here are examples of ways mediators can begin creating dialogue opportunities with people in narrow target markets:

- A mediator focusing on small- to mid-size businesses sponsors a chamber of commerce mixer. As a sponsor, the mediator has the opportunity to speak briefly about her business and offer to serve—right then and there—as an on-the-spot resource for attendees who'd like to chat after the mediator wraps up her welcome remarks.

- A divorce mediator who specializes in high-conflict, post-divorce work decides to build relationships with counselors and therapists as referral sources. That mediator joins an open-membership psychological or counseling association and begins regularly attending conferences and meetings.

- A construction mediator writes a regular "Ask a Mediator" column in a trade publication, inviting readers to e-mail their questions. Some questions are suitable for future columns, and some lead to private work.

- A mediator interested in microbusinesses sponsors free monthly "coffee and chat" gatherings with other microbusiness owners. The gatherings are an informal opportunity for microbusiness owners and solo-preneurs to support and learn from one another, and the mediator serves as facilitator/convener.

- A family mediator serves as a parenting resource by sending copies of newspaper or magazine articles to people she's met in her target market. Those clippings prompt telephone thanks from the recipients and provide a few moments of conversation.

- The same mediator serves as a parenting resource by maintaining a comprehensive referral list of area professionals that single parents and blended families could rely on for other needs. The list includes counseling and therapy professionals, teen programs, after-school programs, and driving schools. People actually leave comments on her Web site, requesting her leads for their needs, and she follows up with a short e-mail exchange.

What opportunities can you create to meet, serve, support, inform, and build conversation with your target market?

Online Dialogue

The challenge of in-person dialogue is that you have only one mouth and one set of ears.

Conversing with more than a few people at once is impossible to do well, so you're limited to how many people you can reach in person.

Online is different.

Online, you can write, record, or videocast one question, one idea, or one article, and the number of people who can engage it is virtually unlimited. Unlike a print newsletter, brochure, or marketing flyer, your online material can stay online indefinitely, continuing to attract new readers, new viewers, or new listeners. Online material serves you exponentially in ways that print material cannot.

The Pew Internet and American Life Project has offered their research to confirm what many of us already suspected:

> The Internet has become increasingly important to users in their everyday lives. It is also the case that for many of online Americans, the Internet has become a crucial source of information at major moments and milestones in their lives.

> Our surveys show that 45% of Internet users, or about 60 million Americans, say that the Internet helped them make big decisions or negotiate their way through major episodes in their lives in the previous two years.

And that was several years ago.

So let's look at leveraging your time and energy with online tools for mediation marketing.

How will you tap online tools to help people choose mediation for some of the "major episodes" in their lives?

Blogging for Business

What makes you return to a Web site? Most people return to a site because it does one or more of the following:

- It's informative on a topic of interest.
- It helps solve a problem.
- It entertains.
- It offers an original perspective unavailable elsewhere.

The best ways for you to create opportunities for dialogue with your market, then, are for you to do one or more of the above with your own website.

Blogs are an increasingly popular way to carry that off.

Blogs are not different than websites. Blogs *are* websites. A particular type of website.

A blog is a type of website that organizes information in a specific way, makes the information easily syndicated, and incorporates a tool for interaction with visitors to your site. I'm betting you've visited many blogs even if you were unaware they were blogs. They're that prevalent, and they tend to show up high in the results of online searches.

Blogs have come a long way from days when their primary use was for teenagers to share their personal journals online. And as businesses from Fortune 500 companies to solo-preneurs join in, it's clear they're not just a fad. As marketing tools, they are effective for some very powerful reasons:

- Good blogs deliver fresh, unique content that creates search engine fodder and gets human visitors to return. Each return creates a chance for relationship, trust, and conversation to build.

- You don't need to be a geek to blog. If you have an Internet connection and can learn a bit of software that's almost as easy as email, you can use blog software to organize, manage, and promote your Web site. With blogging, you're not dependent on a web designer to make changes and keep your site up-to-date.

- Blogging is cost effective. The software costs virtually nothing (and sometimes literally nothing), and the look and layout of a blog can be changed, at low or no cost, to make your blog reflect your voice, your image, and your brand.

And the public is catching on, big time. According to the Pew Internet and American Life Project, "by the end of 2004, blogs had established themselves as a key part of online culture." For instance,

- Blog readership shot up an eye-popping 58 percent in 2004. Over six million Americans got news and information fed to them through RSS aggregators (the technology that makes reading blogs a cinch—more on this later).

- Twenty-seven percent of Internet users said they read blogs, a 58-percent jump from the 17 percent only eleven months prior. This translates into 32 million Americans who were blog readers by the end of 2004.

- Twelve percent of Internet users have posted comments or other material on blogs, suggesting that the public is starting to catch on to the idea of interacting with websites.

The *Boston Globe* has noted that an effective online presence is essential for career development:

- Blogging makes self-employment easier. You can't make it on your own unless you're good at marketing yourself. One of the most cost-effective and efficient ways of marketing yourself is with a blog. When someone searches for your product or service, make sure your blog comes up first.

- Blogging provides more opportunities. Building brands, changing careers, launching a business—these endeavors are much easier once you've established yourself online.

- Blogging creates a network. A blogger puts himself out in the world as someone who is interesting and engaging—just the type of person everyone wants to meet.

How Blogging Helps You Market

If you want to create dialogue with prospective clients, then you need places for that dialogue to begin. In today's wired world, blogs are one of the terrific tools for the job:

Blogs help people find you. Because search engines seem to love blogs, people seeking information or support on a topic that you write about have a better chance of finding you (again, if you've focused your market and niche sufficiently) when you use blogging software. And with the growth in "local search," the use of a search engine to find services or businesses near you—even when the phone book's in the next room—having a findable web presence matters more than ever.

Blogging brings people back to your site. When you focus your online presence on your market's most important interests, they come back, because the technology built into blogging software and related e-mail notification services make it easy for them to know what's new. When you post to a blog, the blog helps do the notifying for you.

Blogging showcases your personality, your knowledge, and your relevance. When you write for any length of time on a subject, you convey staying power, commitment to your work, expertise, and experience. Because blogs make it easy for visitors to see the depth of your knowledge, by showcasing your articles in simple lists and archives that are already built into the software, your well-done blog whispers, "Hey, stick around for a bit. This person's got some credibility." You could do this with a static Web site, though usually with a lot more effort to make it work as well as blogs will do it.

Blogs convey approachability. Because the writing in blogs is usually more informal than other forms of professional writing (such as journals), the well-crafted blog reaches out and touches the reader. Because blog posts tend to be brief, blogs make it convenient to consume and digest information in bite-sized chunks. Picture yourself attending a soiree and walking up to a person who speaks for minutes on end without pausing or inviting you into the conversation. Do you want to spend more time with that person, or do you want to talk to the person who shares a thought or two on a subject and then invites your thoughts? This is also possible with a static site, but will typically require more effort to pull off.

Blogs help start conversation. As I mentioned before, skilled inquiry and careful listening are hallmarks of effective dialogue. Blogs create an online opportunity not just for clients to "listen" to you but also for you to engage your client.

Blogs do this through the built-in comments feature that's part of blogging software and through other mechanisms now common on any good website—contact forms, short surveys and reader polls, ask-a-question forms, and even discussion forums.

Blogs help build a referral network. I regularly refer past, current, and prospective clients to other credible blogs with information relevant to their needs and interests. Other bloggers do the same for me. The blogosphere is a generally hospitable place where the old, fixed-pie, self-protective, "don't let them leave your site once you've got them there" paradigm is giving way to the new, expanded-pie, generous, "show them where else they can find useful information, and they'll remember you with gratitude." Most business bloggers recognize and benefit from this referral network and regularly take part.

Static Website or Blog?

If you know the song, *Anything You Can Do,* hum it along with Annie Oakley and me now:

Anything you can do,
I can do better.
I can do anything
Better than you.

That's a blog singing to a static website.

Static websites are similar to online brochures. The simplest version has a home page that welcomes the visitor, a page or several pages describing services, perhaps links to a few articles, frequently asked questions, contact information, and the like. If you have this type of website, you intend it primarily to be informational, and you probably update it only occasionally.

They're a dying breed. As they should be. It's time. They've done their service, and there are new kids in town.

Blogs can do anything a static site can do. And more.

A blog makes use of a syndication feature that helps readers know of new information without any effort on your part. Articles, called posts, are typically listed in reverse chronological order, so your freshest material is on view first when a visitor arrives on your main blog page. Blogs can have both "posts" (articles) and "pages" (static pages with information about the creator, contact information, testimonials, etc.).

Blogging software allows you to categorize posts by topic and timeline so that visitors interested in a specific subtopic or a period in time can find your articles easily. While this is also possible with a static website, blogging software makes this categorizing and organizing as simple as the single click of your mouse button.

Perhaps most important, blogs have a feature that makes them highly relevant for dialogue marketing: they invite the reader to interact with what's written. Most bloggers want to hear from readers. While the majority of readers don't leave comments, as business blogging catches on, more and more people understand that the blogger relies on comments to direct what to write about. Comments let the blogger know what resonated most with the readers, what questions they still have, and what confused them or stopped them short.

Some of my best clients have come to me via comments left on one of my business blogs. The comments turned out to be the start of a conversation that went somewhere compelling.

How can you turn your dusty, static website into a dialogue-generating engine for your business? How can you create a compelling conversation with your site?

Static Website *and* Blog?

Let's imagine that your business name is Dispute Resolution Services for Cat Owners (well, you've done a fine job of choosing a focused target market, I'll give you that). You've had a static website and now wish to tap the opportunities created by blogging.

Do you replace your static website with a blog-based site? Or leave your static site as is and link to your new blog?

Many business owners have chosen to integrate a blog with their static site by creating a link to the blog from the site's home or other pages. The benefit of this approach is the simplicity of leaving your static site alone but for adding a single link, an option that may be appealing if you've recently paid a handsome sum for your static site's design. The downside of this approach is that, without additional design help, it's unlikely you'll find it easy to visually integrate the two; your static site is likely to have one look and your blog quite another. With the use of similar graphics and colors, you may be able to reduce the visual gap.

With the "linked but separate" approach, you'll also need to make a decision about naming or branding your blog. You have, essentially, three choices:

- Your blog and your static Web site share the same title, which may or may not be the same as your business name.

- Your blog's title is the same as your static site with "Blog" at the end.

- Your blog's title is different but associated with your static site's name.

Let's return to Dispute Resolution Services for Cat Owners to illustrate these options. With the first option, both the main static site and blog could feature the business name. With the second, the blog's title would be The Dispute Resolution Services for Cat Owners Blog (or DRSCO Blog, I suppose). That's starting to become quite a mouthful and doesn't exactly roll off the tongue. A few people have mixed or downright negative feelings about including the word "Blog" in a title because of blogging's roots in teenage journal angst.

The third alternative is to name your blog something like "Purrfect Harmony." It's separate and distinct from your static site, yet clearly related, and the visitor to your blog can probably guess that you write something about cats or cat owners, and getting along.

I predict that in a few years, you'll no longer need to make the decision to convert your entire site to a blog platform or keep your blog as a separate entity. As more and more of us convert our entire sites, I believe the trend will evolve into all Web sites naturally integrating the special features of blog platforms—or whatever they mature into over time.

If you don't yet have a static website or have one that's getting a bit long in the tooth, your best option is probably to create a new site using blogging software.

Several years ago I converted my static business sites to a blogsite, as I have with MakingMediationYourDayJob.com I want visitors from my target markets-to see new material right away, without having to click through one or more links to see what's fresh. I also want visitors to be able to find out other traditional information (who I am, how to contact me, etc.) easily. And I want the ease and simplicity of managing content for my site without a lot of effort. Blog software does all of this.

How you structure your own site along the static-blog continuum is a decision that needs to combine your personal preferences with the needs of the target market you're trying to cultivate. Here are some questions to consider:

- Do you want customer-focused content front and center? Then a blog-based site is a good choice.

- Do you want your customers to first learn more about you and what you're selling? You can do this with either a static or a blog-based site, since blogs can have static pages just like a static Web site.

- Do you want articles to be an add-on but not a central feature of your site? Then a static site, from which you offer a link to our blog, can work, though you can accomplish the same with a blog-based site that uses what's called a "static home page."

- Are you website design and HTML savvy, or do you have cash in hand to pay a site designer? If not, then a blogsite is much simpler to get going. If so, spend it on having a blog-based site designed to match your business brand.

- Do you have the ability or the funds to coordinate the appearances of your static site and your blog site, so they relate to one another in spirit and design? If not, then selecting a blog platform for your Web site is likely a solid choice.

Podcasts

There's a bigger world out there than just blogs these days.

Podcasts are audio broadcasts that have been converted to a file type accessible from the Internet. Podcasts can be streamed from a computer connected to the Internet, downloaded for later listening, or added to a portable music player for listening on the go.

Many Podcasts are free, just like most blogs, and getting new Podcasts works much like receiving notification of new blog posts. For instance, I use iTunes, a free, downloadable software program for PCs and Macs. I can visit the iTunes store online, browse the hundreds of available Podcasts by category, and click a button to subscribe. Whenever I open iTunes in the future, the software automatically checks to see if that subscription has any new Podcasts; if so, they're downloaded automatically. If I connect my portable audio player, iTunes automatically places the new Podcasts there as well. I store them up for listening on my morning run or during long car, train, and plane travels.

If you're more comfortable and more effective talking than writing, then podcasting may be a realistic option. You'll need to create an audio broadcast, which can be done with a computer-connected microphone or with free (or low-cost) teleconferencing services that allow you to call in and record, then save your digital audio file. You may find it helpful to have an audio editing program, some of which are available at reasonable cost and even free. And you'll need a place for your Podcasts to reside on the Internet. There are services that make this a cinch, and you can also make your Podcasts available from your website or blogsite.

Mediators who Podcast to reach their target market can cover content very similar to a good business blog, and then some. For instance, you can:

- Record your opening statement so that potential mediation clients get a fuller understanding of what might happen at the table.

- Have someone interview you about what happens in the mediation room, including information such as myths and realities.

- Interview a member of your target audience who has made successful use of mediation.

- Record your answers to questions about ADR, mediation and other topics that are commonly asked by members of your target audience.

The companion site for this book, which you can find by visiting MakingMediationYourDayJob.com, has a list of free ADR-related Podcasts you can sample.

Video Blogs

Also called vBlogs and vlogs, video blogs are essentially blogs with video clips instead of, or as a supplement to, print. As more computer users have access to broadband Internet, streaming video is gaining popularity.

You'll need a bit more technology to produce a vlog than a blog, though it's not complicated technology and some of it is now bundled with software already on your computer when you purchase it. You'll need technology to make a short video clip—a computer, a camcorder that records digitally, or a digital camera capable of recording moving as well as still pictures. You'll need some editing software, which is now bundled automatically with many new computers, including both Macs and PCs.

You'll also need a place for your videos to reside on the Internet, preferably on your own site or connected seamlessly with your own site, since you want your vlog to be associated with you (linking to and from YouTube, for example), not the service that's streaming it for viewers.

Much like blogging and podcasting, content for vlogs should focus on video your target audience would appreciate and find useful. Depending on your audience, you might include items such as:

- A short clip of your mediation room or offices, to show people what a mediation meeting room looks like.

- A clip of you answering common reader/viewer questions.

- A clip of you talking informally (but without jargon!) about the ways mediation meets people's interests.

- A welcome video for anyone new to your site.

- Interviews with people relevant to your target audience, perhaps even former clients.

It's a Fast-Moving World

All of the technology tools I've discussed so far are old hat in the tech world. Blogs, for example, have been around since the turn of the millennium.

More recently we've seen wikis, Twitter, and tumblelogs. I might as well be speaking Vulcan, right?

Don't worry about keeping up. Worry about building dialogue and following a few key resources that do a good job of keeping you informed of what's new and worth your attention.

In the meantime, here are a few more online tools for meeting up with and talking to people in your target market (with the perhaps obvious caveat that you'll want to make sure members of your market are using these before you dive in):

E-zines. E-zines are online newsletters delivered digitally to your mailing list. They're much less expensive to produce and send than a print newsletter, and they're common now. With an e-zine service, some of which are free and most of which are reasonably priced, you can create your e-zine with relative ease (or use one you've paid someone to design for you), send it out on the date you specify with the ease of a button click, and ensure you're staying in compliance with laws intended to reduce e-mail spam.

Blog, e-zine, or both? There are strong opinions all over the map on this one. Some say blogs are still too new for marketers to give up e-zines and newsletters. Others say that since people can subscribe to blogs by e-mail, there's no particular need to produce a newsletter too—it's a lot of writing time. Still others say that you can use blog posts for your newsletter or newsletter articles for your blog and so do both easily.

Forget what everybody else says. Do what makes sense for you and, more important, for your target market. Ask a few members of your target market to help you decide. Take your own time into account. As one mediator said to me, "I want to blog in order to build business. I don't want blogging to *become* my business."

Discussion Forums. If some or all of your target market is Internet savvy, they may make use of online discussion forums for some of the problems they face. For instance, 55-Alive.com is an online community for people over the age of 55 looking to lead vibrant retirement lives. If you're a mediator interested in working with an elderly target market or on elderly issues, then joining such a site helps you gain a better understanding of that audience needs and helps you join discussions with that audience.

Social Networking Sites. MySpace and Facebook conjure images of teens and twentysomethings talking about their social lives. If you work with these populations, then you sure want to learn more about these social networking sites! But even if you don't, these sites are seeing increases in use by adults looking to create professional and social networks. They're not just for teens anymore. For a more buttoned-down professional networking site, check LinkedIn. Or to create your own social network without joining any of the above three, there's Ning. And, of course, dozens more. But my intention isn't to overwhelm you by listing them all!

One closing thought: Don't try to do them all, at least at the start. Talk to your market, find out what they follow, what they like, what they find intrusive or annoying. It'll keep you sane.

Reflective Question 7.1
What marketing activities create opportunities for dialogue?

This exercise invites you to align potential marketing tasks with ways to create learning conversations with people in your market. Create a free-form list of activities that are either naturally based on dialogue or open the door effectively for dialogue to happen. I suggest that you return to this activity several times over the coming days, as more ideas are likely to occur while this chapter incubates in your mind.

Reflective Question 7.2
How would you initiate dialogue?

Pick one of the target markets you've identified, then play another game of imagination: where would you go to engage your potential clients in the kinds of dialogue you think would capture their interest and help them solve a compelling problem?

Begin by considering location. Where would you go to meet and speak with them? Where would you send information to follow up your in-person engagement? How would you make use of the Internet to reach out to them?

Then consider how you'd engage them in dialogue. If you think you'd like to give a presentation, how would you turn it into dialogue? If you think you'd like to mail them your brochure, how would you turn it into dialogue? If you'd like them to visit your Web site, how would you turn that visit into dialogue? Press yourself to answer this question, as therein lies the key to unlocking your marketing potential.

Reflective Question 7.3
How can you create return visitors to your Web site?

With your target market in mind, write out your answers to the following questions. Try to avoid generalist answers that would fit any market (*e.g.*, "Tell them about mediation"). Instead, try to speak directly to their interests. If you're not sure, select ten key stakeholders from your target market and ask them how they'd answer these questions. In return for their time, consider a gift certificate for their favorite coffee joint, or some other light thank-you gift.

- What topics *most* interest them? How could you be an information resource on one or more of those topics? Consider topics that aren't only conflict-related.

- What problems do they specifically have? What could you write about that helps them solve these problems without giving all your talent away?

- What kinds of things entertain people in your target market? How could you use a Web site to entertain in that way?

- What can you offer them that isn't just a restating of someone else's work or ideas? In other words, what would make you unique to your ideal audience?

- Would they be most interested in information they could read, listen to, or watch? Or do they prefer some combination of the three?

- What kind of information would make them interested in placing their e-mail address on your private mailing list? What would get in the way?

CHAPTER 8

Setting Your
Practice-Building Agenda

When you're Mediating, if the parties reach resolution, you would not usually get up, wish them well, and simply leave the room. Instead, you'd typically help them capture the details of that agreement for future reference.

The act of writing down their agreement helps parties finalize important details, co-create an image of the future, and identify next steps for moving forward on their plan.

Similarly, I'm inviting you not to metaphorically leave the room before your marketing effort is synthesized into actions you can take to move you forward now. I want to take the work you've been doing in the book and assist you in translating it into action … action you can look forward to taking!

So it's time to create your action plan for the next ninety days. Before you begin drafting your simple and concise plan, review your responses to all of the exercises in the book. Refresh your memory and mark responses and ideas that stand out to you as particularly compelling.

Go ahead, take fifteen to twenty minutes to do it now. I'll wait.

A One-Page Plan

Let's not create a tome of a plan. Tomes intimidate and cry out to be shelved and left alone. Who wants to carry around a tome?

Instead, I invite you to create a one-page plan that will span only the next ninety days. It shouldn't be a plan that is full to the brim with all you wish to accomplish to launch your business into Thrivingville. It should be a plan that's pared down to three or four major goals that move you forward. Simply that: move you forward.

It will be a plan built on marketing tasks you enjoy, with a market about which you feel passion and that leverages the jump-start you've given yourself by completing this book's exercises.

I recommend these sections and have provided samples on the companion website for this book (see the Bonus Material section later in this chapter for more information):

Your Target Market. A very concise description of your target market and where you can locate them. Use your responses to Chapter 4 questions to guide you.

Your Primary Services and Roles. A list of the services you will offer, and the roles you will play in order to be a mediative influence in your target market. Use your responses to Chapter 6 questions to guide you.

Your Dialogue-Building Strategy. A paragraph describing what approaches you will use to build dialogue with your target market. Use your responses to Chapter 7 questions to guide you.

Your Top Three Goals and Next Actions. Identify three goals you can reach in the next ninety days and a single action to get you started with each goal. Make them achievable, not such a far reach that you aren't likely to do them. I encourage one goal of each type: an in-person strategy, a technology-based strategy, and a print-based strategy.

At the end of ninety days, review your one-page plan and create a new one for the following ninety days. And so on. Big plans balanced by bite-sized chunks will create momentum.

What's the Next Action?

If you've read David Allen's time- and project-management bestseller, *Getting Things Done*, then you're already be familiar with the concept of "next action." Allen proposes that one way to become masterful in moving forward with your goals is to use the critical question, "What's the next action?"

The next action is your next physical, concrete activity that moves a goal or project toward completion. Allen uses this example to illustrate the subtle but important difference between naming an objective or problem, and identifying a next action:

> For example, a client will have something like "tires" on a list.
> I then ask, "What's that about?
> He responds, "Well, I need new tires on my car."
> "So what's the next action?"
> At that point the client usually wrinkles up his forehead, ponders for a few moments, and expresses his conclusion: "Well, I need to call a tire store and get some prices."
> That's about how much time is required to decide what the "doing" would be like on almost everything. It's just the few seconds of focused thinking that most people have not yet done about most of their stuff."

I like Allen's approach because it helps take large tasks or big goals and break them into manageable, bite-sized chunks. While "Build a Web site" is vague and daunting, "Sign up with a web host that offers one-click installations of Word-Press" (an excellent, free blogging software program) is specific and achievable.

Should You Have a Business Plan?

In Chapter 2 I referenced a Small Business Development Center director who gave me two pieces of valuable advice that still serve me today. Now I'll tell you about his second piece of advice: Write a business plan.

That was a daunting notion for me at the time because I'd never done one before and couldn't completely comprehend why I needed one without the intention to seek startup funding support. I decided to give it an initial pass, see if it looked like it would be a helpful process, and then finish the plan if it proved valuable. It was one of the most valuable activities in my first months in business.

I don't believe that everyone should write a formal business plan, though I do believe that every mediator who hopes to build a thriving business must think strategically about his or her business. Crafting some or all of a business plan can help you do this because:

- It will force you to think methodically through critical aspects of your ADR business and create a foundation for all your other activities.

- It will leave you with written language you can use later for marketing and other efforts.

- It will teach you the basics of business accounting and guide you in determining your likely billable hours, your fees, your decisions about overhead expenses, and what you'll need to stay afloat and thrive.

- It will cause you to research your competition and identify where there are holes in the market that you can fill.

If you elect to write down your plan, your finished product may not need to include everything typically involved in a formal business plan. The most valuable sections are likely to be the ones that make you reflect deeply on and perhaps conduct a bit of research about your ADR business. Key topics for any mediation practice, whether you're newly formed or have been in business for a while, include:

Business vision and mission: Why am I doing this? What community needs will the business meet, and how do I know that?

Business goals: Why am I choosing to be in business? How will I know I'm successful? What are my short-term and long-term success goals?

Business support: In what business ownership areas do I need support and resources to be successful (financial, technical, strategic, etc.)?

Business services: What specific services will I offer, and how will I describe them? How do I know there's both a need for and interest in those services?

Competition: Who are my three primary competitors, and what are their strengths and weaknesses? How will I differentiate myself from them? What are my business strengths and weaknesses as compared to my competitors? What does my competition charge for services?

Markets: What are the characteristics of my target markets? What are their sizes and locations? How will members of my target markets learn about and buy my services?

Marketing and promotion: How will I promote my services? How will I use print, audio, and digital media most effectively? What will those efforts cost in terms of financial outlay and my time?

Financials: What are my proposed fees? How do I know they're both in the range of what the market will bear *and* sustainable for my business? What are my overhead expenses? What are my financial resources for backup during the startup phases of my business? How many monthly billable hours do I need to cover expenses and earn my desired income?

If you've completed the exercises in this book, then you've already taken a respectable first pass at the business vision/mission, business goals, business services, markets, and marketing and promotion sections. The act of writing out your plan will help you synthesize it into actions.

I still maintain a written business and marketing plan, which I update annually. It doesn't look like the kind of formal plan you'd submit to a bank, foundation, or other funding source, but it covers, in detail, all of the sections above.

This kind of methodical and reflective annual tradition has become something I look forward to, because it grounds me again in choosing the Important over the Urgent.

The Thousand-Link Crossing

When I was a mediation student studying at Woodbury College (where I now serve on the graduate faculty), I had the tremendous good fortune of learning from some of the best mediators in the United States, if not the world. Among them was Susanne Terry, someone I still consider a mentor and am lucky now to call a friend.

One day in class, Susanne shared a story she's given me permission to share now with you.

The Thousand-Link Crossing

Once upon a time there were two men standing beside the riverbank, loudly arguing. They shouted at each other with increasing anger until at last it appeared that each might do harm to the other.

About that time, as these things happen, a woman came from the nearby woods and inquired about what was happening. "Why are you shouting?" she said. "Why are your faces bunched up and mean?"

They each told her that they were fighting over the boat that was on the shore beside them. It seems that many years ago they had bought the boat together and used it to fish the river. They would feed their families with the fish and then sell what fish were left over. Now their children were grown, and the men fished less often. Over time, they explained to the woman, there were disagreements about who used the boat the most, who repaired it most frequently, and who took better care of it. Now those disagreements had caused the two to barely be able to speak to one another, much less use the boat together.

The woman asked "But what are you arguing about right now?"

"Ah," one of the men said, "the problem is that we both have to cross this wide river, and obviously I cannot ride in the boat with this fool."

"I certainly will not ride with this foolish person," the other one added, "and we don't know how one can take the boat across and the other can also cross. Neither of us is willing to let the other one take the boat until that is solved."

"Oh" the woman said, "I wonder if I have something that may help?" With that she pulled from a large bag some tools and beautiful pieces of metal. Each piece of metal glittered, appeared to be made of gold, and was hard to the touch. However, each piece weighed almost nothing, as did the entire bundle of beautiful metal pieces.

"What do you suppose we could do with these?" she puzzled.

"Ah-ha, I have it," one said. "These pieces of metal can be shaped and put together in order to form a chain. This chain can be attached to the boat."

The other man added, "The boat can cross carrying one of us. The other one can pull the boat back to his side of the river using the chain."

The woman nodded and the men thought about this. "Of course, in order to make the chain, we'd have to have some way to heat each of the pieces of metal so that they could be bent. Is that possible?"

"Yes, certainly," the men said, setting out to find what was needed to start a fire. One brought dry leaves and twigs, the other, sticks and branches. The woman provided a piece of flint to light the fire, which was soon roaring.

The woman showed the men how to take each piece of metal, place it in the fire and bend it. To do this, one man would hold the last link made, and the other would insert the heated piece of metal through the link. When it was in place, the woman would ask if they were ready. When each man had said yes, the woman, using her tools, bent the ends of the metal together to make a new link.

And so the work went. Hour after hour, the metal was heated and was inserted through the link. Each time, the woman said "Now? Are you ready?" Each time, the men said yes, and a new link was formed.

After a bit, the men grew tired and hungry and had begun quarreling again. Finally, the woman said. "We are indeed hungry. It would be so good if we could eat something. I have a pot with me but there seems to be nothing to put in it. Do you suppose we could find something?"

"Certainly," the men said and immediately one offered a turnip and two potatoes from his knapsack. The other, after only a few moments, gave a piece of sausage. Soon there was a stew boiling in the pot.

After they had eaten, the woman said. "Oh my, you are so tired. It is a shame that there is no way for you to rest. Could that happen?"

One of the men said to the other, "Of course it is possible. All we have to do is lie down and sleep for a bit." And so they did, while the woman tended the fire. After they were refreshed by both the food and fire, the three resumed their work.

After another while, the woman said to the men. "We have placed one thousand links in this chain. I wonder if it is enough. Look at the chain and look at the river. Is the chain long enough to span the river, so that it can pull your boat back?"

The men consulted with one another, measured, and remeasured the chain. Eventually they said, "Yes, the chain is now long enough."

"Do you suppose you can cross now?" the woman asked. "Certainly" the men responded.

"Is it time?" she asked. The men consulted with one another and then agreed that it was time to cross the river.

With that the woman gathered up the thousand-link chain and dumped it into her bag. "Good-bye" she said. "You have done well." Then she walked away into the woods.

And the two men got into their boat and rowed to the other side.

What first few links will you put in your marketing chain?

Bonus Material

I want to give you a gift for purchasing this book and giving me the opportunity to help you jump-start your mediation business: supporting and newer material that I couldn't include here.

Please visit MakingMediationYourDayJob.com, where you'll find message boards open to everyone and reader-only material you can access using passwords I've created from passages in this book.

There's material there now, waiting for you, and I'll add more over time as I hear back from readers like you.

Closing Words and Wishes

Thanks for joining me on this journey to making mediation your day job. I look forward to the day you and many other good mediators have built thriving practices doing what you love, which will surely benefit our communities and world. I look forward to the day your marketing efforts become enjoyable because you're seeing real results. And I look forward to the day there's real momentum in our field because we've understood what our markets really want and need.

I'm glad if I played a small part in such days coming to pass for you. I hope you'll keep in touch and let me know (Tammy@Lenski.com).

Best to you in bringing your ADR dreams to life,

Tammy

Recommended Resources

Books on Marketing

Beckwith, H. (1997). *Selling the invisible: A field guide to modern marketing*. New York: Warner Books.

Godin, S. (2002). *Purple cow*. New York: Penguin Group.

Heath, C., & Heath, D. (2007). *Made to stick: Why some ideas survive and others die*. New York: Random House.

McLellan, D. (2003). *99.3 random acts of marketing*. Des Moines, IA: Innova Training & Consulting.

Port, M. (2006). *Book yourself solid*. Hoboken, NJ: John Wiley & Sons, Inc.

Wolter, R. (2006). *Kickstart your success*. Hoboken, NJ: John Wiley & Sons, Inc.

Books on Social Media

Scoble, R., & Israel, S. (2006). *Naked conversations: How blogs are changing the way businesses talk with customers*. Hoboken, NJ: John Wiley & Sons, Inc.

Sernovitz, A. (2006). *Word of mouth marketing*. Chicago: Kaplan.

VanFossen, L. (2007). *Blogging tips: What bloggers won't tell you about blogging*. London: SplashPress.

Wibbels, A. (2006). *Blogwild! A guide for small business blogging*. New York: Penguin Group.

Books on Managing Your Life or Business

Allen, D. (2001). *Getting things done: The art of stress-free productivity*. New York: Penguin Group.

Covey. S. R. (1989). *The 7 habits of highly effective people*. New York: Simon & Schuster.

Gerber, M. (1995). *The e-myth revisited: Why most small businesses don't work and what to do about it*. New York: HarperCollins.

Godin, S. (2007). *The dip: A little book that teaches you when to quit (and when to stick)*. New York: Penguin Group.

Nemeth, M. (1997) *The energy of money: A spiritual guide to financial and personal fulfillment*. New York: Ballantine Publishing Group.

Trapani, G. (2007). *Lifehacker: 88 tech tips to turbocharge your day*. Indianapolis: Wiley Publishing, Inc.

Books on the ADR Field and Careers

Bowling, D., & Hoffman, D. (Eds.). (2003). *Bringing peace into the room: How the personal qualities of the mediator impact the process of conflict resolution*. San Francisco: Jossey-Bass.

Mayer, B. S. (2004). *Beyond neutrality: Confronting the crisis in conflict resolution*. San Francisco: Jossey-Bass.

Mosten, F. (2001). *The mediation career guide: A strategic approach to building a successful practice*. San Francisco: Jossey-Bass.

Recommended Online Resources

For my latest, hot-off-the-presses, up-to-date recommended online resources list, visit MakingMediationYourDayJob.com.

References

Introduction

Beer, J. E., & Stief, E. (1997). *The mediator's handbook*. British Columbia: New Society Publishers.

Mayer, B. S. (2004). *Beyond neutrality: Confronting the crisis in conflict resolution*. San Francisco: Jossey-Bass.

Chapter 1

Komives, S. R. (2000, November–December). Inhabit the gap. *About Campus*, 31–32.

Chapter 2

Bowling, D. & Hoffman, D. A. (2003). *Bringing peace into the room: How the personal qualities of the mediator impact the process of conflict resolution*. San Francisco: Jossey-Bass.

Howell, W. C., & Fleishman, E. A. (Eds.). (1982). *Human performance and productivity*, 2. Hillsdale, NJ: Erlbaum.

Chapter 3

Covey, S. R. (1989). *The 7 habits of highly effective people: Powerful lessons in personal change.* New York: Simon & Schuster.

Ferriss, T. (2007). *The 4-hour workweek.* New York: Crown Publishers.

Wolter, R. (2006). *Kick-start your success: Four powerful steps to get what you want out of your life, career and business.* Hoboken, NJ: John Wiley & Sons.

Chapter 4

AtKisson, A. (2002). *Believing Cassandra: An optimist looks at a pessimist's world.* New York: Scribe.

Ferriss, T. (2007). *The 4-hour workweek.* New York: Crown Publishers.

Gladwell, M. (2002). *The tipping point: How little things can make a big difference.* New York: Back Bay Books.

Godin, S. (2002). *Unleashing the ideavirus.* New York: Simon & Schuster.

Chapter 5

Douglas, L. C. (December 2000). *Marketing features vs. benefits: Learn the difference, and then see the difference in your bottom line.* Retrieved February 2, 2006, from http://www.entrepreneur.com/magazine/homeofficemagcom/2000/december/34942.html.

Moore, C. W. (1996). *The mediation process: Practical strategies for resolving conflict.* San Francisco: Jossey-Bass.

Ury, W. (1991). *Getting past no: Negotiating your way from confrontation to cooperation.* New York: Bantam.

Chapter 6

Mayer, B. S. (2000). *The dynamics of conflict resolution: A practitioner's guide.* San Francisco: Jossey-Bass.

Mayer, B. S. (2004). *Beyond neutrality: Confronting the crisis in conflict resolution.* San Francisco: Jossey-Bass.

Port, M. (2006). *Book yourself solid: The fastest, easiest, and most reliable system for getting more clients than you can handle even if you hate marketing and selling.* Hoboken, NJ: John Wiley & Sons.

Suzuki, D. T. (1970). *Zen mind, beginner's mind: Informal talks on Zen meditation and practice.* New York: Weatherhill.

Ury, W. (1991). *Getting past no: Negotiating your way from confrontation to cooperation.* New York: Bantam.

Wolter, R. (2006). *Kick-start your success: Four powerful steps to get what you want out of your life, career and business.* Hoboken, NJ: John Wiley & Sons.

Chapter 7

Horrigan, J., & Rainie, L. (2006). *The internet's growing role in life's major decisions.* Retrieved June 22, 2006, from http://www.pewinternet.org/PPF/r/181/report_display.asp.

Israel, S. (October 2004). "Conversational marketing." *It Seems to Me.* Retrieved October 12, 2006, from http://seems2shel.typepad.com/itseemstome/2004/10/conversational_.html.

Locke, C., Levine, R., Doc Searls, D., & Weinberger, D. (2001). *The cluetrain manifesto: The end of business as usual.* New York: Perseus.

Rainie, L. (January 2005). *The state of blogging.* Retrieved April 4, 2005, from http://www.pewinternet.org/pdfs/PIP_blogging_data.pdf.

Yankelovich, D. (1999). *The magic of dialogue: Transforming conflict into cooperation*. New York: Touchstone.

Chapter 8

Allen, D. (2002). Getting things done: *The art of stress-free productivity*. New York: Penguin.

Terry, S. (1997). *The thousand-link crossing*. Unpublished manuscript.

CPSIA information can be obtained at www.ICGtesting.com
Printed in the USA
BVOW061306160512

290378BV00003B/31/P

9 781935 278887